Navigating Nonprofit Leadership
a CEO's Guide

By Alan H. Turner II, M.B.A.

Copyright © 2024 Alan H. Turner II
All rights reserved.

No part of this publication may be reproduced, distributed, or transmitted in any form or by any means, including photocopying, recording, or other electronic or mechanical methods, without the prior written permission of the publisher, except in the case of brief quotations embodied in reviews and certain other non-commercial uses permitted by copyright law.

ISBN: 9798339795827
Imprint: Independently published

Dedication

To my wife, Stephanie…

Thank you for taking this amazing journey with me.
I can not imagine a life without your love and support.
I love you!

To my children, Andrew and Sara…

Thank you for rolling with all the changes.
You are my biggest achievements.
I love you both!

Table of Contents

Introduction	ix
Chapter 1 : What is a Nonprofit?	1
Chapter 2 : Nonprofit CEO Positions and Essential Skill Sets	11
Chapter 3 : Applying for a Nonprofit CEO Position	21
Chapter 4 : Know Your Organization	31
Chapter 5: The Importance of Relationships	37
Chapter 6: Understanding Your Board	47
Chapter 7: Meetings and Agendas – Your New Best Friend	61
Chapter 8: Know Your Numbers: Budgets and Financials	69
Chapter 9: What is Overhead and Why You Need to Know it?	81

Chapter 10: The Importance of Fundraising	89
Chapter 11: Making an Impact: How to Drive and Demonstrate Success	99
Chapter 12: Lead Your Staff: The Art of Leadership	113
Chapter 13: Getting Your Message Out	123
Chapter 14: The Power of Thank You and Recognition	135
Chapter 15: Mastering Time Management	143
Chapter 16: Taking Care of Yourself	153
Chapter 17: Where Do You Go from Here?	167
Conclusion: Navigating the Journey of Nonprofit Leadership	183
About the Author	193

Introduction:
Navigating Nonprofit Leadership:
a CEO's Guide

When I began my journey in the nonprofit sector over 25 years ago, I had no idea just how complex, rewarding, and at times overwhelming the role of a nonprofit CEO could be. Throughout my career, I've had the privilege of serving with organizations like United Way in South Dakota, Florida, Alabama, and Tennessee, as well as larger entities like the Boy Scouts of America, St. Jude Children's Research Hospital, and the American Red Cross. Each step has taught me something new about the incredible impact nonprofits can have on communities, families, and individuals—and about the unique challenges of leading these organizations.

Over the years, one thing has become abundantly clear: many people are interested in becoming nonprofit CEOs, but lack guidance. Whether they are preparing to apply for their first role or have already stepped into the position, new CEOs often find themselves facing tough questions. How do you manage relationships with board members? How do you navigate complex financial statements? These are questions I've received time and time again, through calls, emails, and impromptu conversations. It's always a pleasure to share what I've learned and help ease the uncertainty for others.

These interactions inspired me to write this book. Navigating Nonprofit Leadership: A CEO's Guide is a collection of insights, advice, and practical tips that I've gathered over my career. It's designed for both aspiring and current nonprofit CEOs—people who want to better understand their roles, tackle the challenges they'll face, and ultimately lead their organizations to success.

Leading a nonprofit isn't just about having a passion for the mission—although that's a huge part of it. It requires a deep understanding of the complexities of nonprofit operations, mastering relationships, and making tough decisions that shape the future of your organization and the people it serves.

In this book, we'll cover the essential topics every nonprofit CEO needs to be familiar with. From understanding what a nonprofit truly is (Chapter 1), to gaining an in-depth knowledge of your organization (Chapter 4), to navigating the perennial challenge of fundraising (Chapter 10), each chapter dives into key areas where I've seen leaders either thrive or struggle.

Chapter 2 explores different types of nonprofit CEO roles and the essential skills needed to lead effectively. If you're preparing to apply for a CEO position, Chapter 3 offers valuable guidance on how to approach that process. Once you're in the role, knowing your numbers (Chapter 8) and understanding overhead (Chapter 9) will be critical for ensuring your organization's long-term sustainability.

But leadership isn't just about operations and finances. In the nonprofit world, relationships matter just as much —if not more. Chapter 5 delves into the importance of building and maintaining strong relationships with staff, donors, volunteers, and partners. In Chapter 6, we'll discuss the unique dynamics between CEOs and their boards, another area where many new leaders often feel unsure. I've also included practical tips on managing meetings and agendas (Chapter 7), which will quickly become your best allies.

As a nonprofit CEO, your ability to inspire, lead, and communicate effectively can make or break your organization's success. That's why I've dedicated chapters to leadership (Chapter 12), getting your message out (Chapter 13), and the importance of gratitude (Chapter 14). Saying "thank you" and recognizing the contributions of your team is more than just good manners—it's essential for fostering a positive organizational culture.

Of course, leadership isn't only about managing others. You must also manage yourself. That's why I've included chapters on mastering time management (Chapter 15) and taking care of yourself (Chapter 16). Leading a nonprofit is demanding, and burnout is a real risk. If you're not careful, the stress and endless to-do lists can take a toll. I've been there, and I want to help you avoid that.

Finally, in Chapter 17, we'll talk about what's next— where do you go from here? Whether you're early in your career or thinking about the horizon, it's important to have a plan. The nonprofit world is full of opportunities, and knowing how to navigate them is key.

This book is intended to be a resource you can refer to at every stage of your nonprofit leadership journey. My goal is to offer practical, experience-based advice. I've had the privilege of leading some remarkable organizations and working with dedicated individuals and teams. Along the way, I've made my share of mistakes. But each challenge has taught me something valuable, and I hope that by sharing these lessons, I can help make your path a little smoother.

Leadership in the nonprofit world is one of the most fulfilling, challenging, and impactful roles you can take on. It requires dedication, adaptability, and a genuine passion for making a difference. I've seen firsthand how strong, compassionate leadership can transform organizations and the communities they serve.

My hope is that this book will serve as a trusted companion as you navigate your own journey as a nonprofit leader. Whether you're preparing to apply for your first CEO role or are already deep into the work, there's always something new to learn.

The nonprofit world is ever-changing, but with the right tools, mindset, and support, you can lead with confidence and make a lasting impact. So let's dive in and start navigating nonprofit leadership together!

Chapter 1: What is a Nonprofit?

When I was growing up, I didn't really understand what a "nonprofit" was. In my family, we didn't use that term. We talked about "charities"—organizations that were there to help people when they needed it most. As a kid, I thought of these groups as simply people helping other people. I didn't see the bigger picture of what was happening behind the scenes.

Each fall, for example, my family would gather extra blankets and take them to the local church for families in need. When my siblings and I outgrew our clothes, those hand-me-downs didn't just sit in our closets— they were donated to people who could use them. Throughout the year, we'd clean out our pantry and collect canned goods we hadn't used. Sometimes, my parents would even shop specifically to buy food for the local food bank. And when Christmas rolled around, ringing the bell for The Salvation Army became a family tradition. I still remember the sound of the bell, the crisp winter air, and the feeling of being part of something bigger. Every time we passed one of those red kettles while out shopping, my dad would hand me some change or a dollar, and I'd happily toss it in.

Looking back, I realize those experiences taught me the importance of giving back and looking out for those who were less fortunate. My parents always reminded us that, no matter how tough we thought we had it, there were people who had it much worse. Some were praying for things we took for granted—like a warm bed, a roof over our heads, food in the pantry, and a loving family.

At the time, I didn't think too much about it beyond the simple act of helping. But as I got older, I began to understand that these acts of charity were just a small part of a much larger world—a world that revolves around nonprofits.

So, What is a Nonprofit, Really?

Nonprofits are everywhere, playing a fundamental role in our society. But the term "nonprofit" can be confusing, and a lot of people misunderstand what it means. When we hear the word "nonprofit," we might think, *Does that mean they don't make any money?* Not quite. The term "nonprofit" doesn't mean the organization can't make money or that it's constantly struggling financially. It simply means that the primary goal of the organization isn't to make a profit for shareholders or owners.

In a typical business, any extra money made after all the bills are paid goes to the owners or shareholders. In a nonprofit, any surplus funds are reinvested back into the organization to help it carry out its mission. The goal isn't to make people rich—it's to make a difference.

Nonprofits come in all shapes and sizes. Some provide essential services like food, shelter, or clothing to people in need. Others focus on issues like education, environmental conservation, or the arts. The diversity of the nonprofit world is one of the things that makes it so special. Every nonprofit has a mission, and each one is working to make the world a better place in its own unique way.

The Many Faces of Nonprofits

When most people think of nonprofits, they picture organizations providing immediate help—like food banks or homeless shelters. But the nonprofit sector is much broader than that. There are nonprofits that work to protect the environment, promote arts and culture, improve healthcare, or advocate for social justice. Some focus on education, offering scholarships or tutoring programs, while others center on animal welfare or disaster relief. There are even nonprofits that exist to support other nonprofits by helping them with things like fundraising or management.

This variety is part of what makes the nonprofit world so interesting. No matter what cause you're passionate about, there's probably a nonprofit out there working on it. And if there isn't, you could even start one!

NGOs: Nonprofits on a Global Scale

You might have heard the term "NGO" (Non-Governmental Organization) and wondered if that's just another word for a nonprofit. The answer is: sort of. NGOs are essentially nonprofits, but the term is more commonly used outside of the United States. NGOs work independently of governments, although they often partner with them or receive government funding. They focus on a range of issues—humanitarian aid, disaster relief, advocacy, and development projects, to name a few. Like nonprofits, NGOs are mission-driven and aren't focused on making a profit.

In many ways, NGOs and nonprofits are cut from the same cloth. Both are dedicated to making the world a better place, and both rely on donations, grants, and other forms of funding to do their work. Whether delivering aid after a disaster, fighting for human rights, or protecting endangered species, NGOs and nonprofits are often at the forefront of the world's most important issues.

Let's Talk About Taxes: The 501(c) Designation

Here's where things get a bit technical, but bear with me—it's important. In the U.S., nonprofits are primarily defined by their tax status. Most people have heard of a "501(c)(3)" organization, but they might not know exactly what it means.

A 501(c)(3) is the most common type of nonprofit designation. These organizations are set up for religious, charitable, scientific, literary, or educational purposes. This designation is important because it allows the organization to be exempt from federal income taxes. Even better, it allows donors to deduct their contributions from their own taxes, which can be a huge incentive for people to give.

But 501(c)(3) isn't the only type of nonprofit. The IRS recognizes over 29 different types of 501(c) organizations. For example, 501(c)(4) organizations are typically social welfare groups—like civic leagues—that might engage in political lobbying. Meanwhile, 501(c)(6) organizations include business leagues or chambers of commerce that promote the interests of their members. This variety allows for a wide range of activities and missions in the nonprofit sector, from advocacy to social services and beyond.

Tax Status is Just Part of the Story

While tax status is important, it doesn't capture the heart of what a nonprofit is. At the end of the day, the most defining feature of a nonprofit is its mission. Nonprofits are created to fill gaps, address societal needs, and advocate for causes that aren't being fully addressed by government or the private sector.

Think about your local food bank. It exists to ensure people in your community don't go hungry. Or consider an organization that advocates for clean water—its mission is to ensure everyone has access to safe drinking water. Whether the nonprofit is small and local or large and international, what drives it forward is its mission to make a difference.

Running a Nonprofit: More Than Just Doing Good

While the heart of a nonprofit is its mission, running a nonprofit is more complex than simply doing good deeds. There are regulations to follow, funding challenges to overcome, and operational demands to manage. Nonprofit leaders wear many hats—they must be experts in fundraising, financial management, strategic planning, and leadership.

One of the biggest challenges in running a nonprofit is balancing the needs of the organization with the expectations of stakeholders—donors, beneficiaries, regulatory bodies, and the community at large. A nonprofit leader must raise funds to keep the organization running, manage the budget responsibly, and ensure that the nonprofit stays on track to achieve its goals—all while keeping everyone happy and engaged.

The Overhead Myth: Why Resources Matter

There's a persistent myth that nonprofits should operate with little to no overhead. The idea is that every dollar donated should go directly to the cause, with nothing spent on administrative costs like salaries or office space. While this sounds noble in theory, the reality is that nonprofits, like any other organization, need resources to function effectively.

Think about it: if a nonprofit can't pay its staff or keep the lights on, how can it fulfill its mission? Nonprofits need well-paid staff, proper technology, and infrastructure to run their programs, expand their impact, and manage day-to-day operations.

The belief that nonprofits should operate on a shoestring budget often leads to burnout among staff, who are overworked and underpaid. It's essential for nonprofit leaders to push back against this myth and advocate for a balanced approach. Operational expenses aren't a waste of money—they're an investment in the organization's capacity to achieve its goals. A well-resourced nonprofit can deliver better programs, serve more people, and ultimately have a greater impact. I will discuss overhead in more detail in Chapter 9.

Accountability and Transparency: The Backbone of Trust

One of the most important aspects of running a nonprofit is being accountable to your stakeholders. Nonprofits are entrusted with donor money and public support, so it's critical that they operate with full transparency. This means being clear about how funds are used, what programs are in place, and the impact being made.

Many nonprofits voluntarily adopt high standards of accountability to build trust with their supporters. This can include regular financial audits, publishing annual reports, and adhering to ethical fundraising practices. These measures help build credibility and demonstrate the nonprofit's commitment to its mission.

Another key aspect of accountability is showing measurable results. Donors want to know their contributions are making a difference, so nonprofits must demonstrate the tangible outcomes of their work. This often involves rigorous monitoring and evaluation processes to track progress against goals. Being transparent about both successes and challenges is key to building long-term relationships with donors and other supporters.

The Role of Advocacy: Nonprofits as Agents of Change

Nonprofits don't just provide direct services; they're also powerful advocates for social change. Whether raising awareness about critical issues or influencing public policy, nonprofits are often the driving force behind important societal shifts. They give a voice to people who might not otherwise be heard and push for laws and policies that benefit the communities they serve.

For example, an environmental nonprofit might lobby for stronger protections for endangered species, while a health nonprofit might advocate for better access to healthcare in underserved communities. In many cases, nonprofit advocacy helps shape the very policies that impact the lives of the people they serve.

Nonprofits and the Economy

You might not think of nonprofits as major economic players, but they are. Nonprofits create jobs, stimulate local economies, and often operate social enterprises—business ventures that generate income to support their mission. These ventures not only provide much-needed services but also create economic opportunities for people who might not otherwise have them.

Did you know that more than 10% of the American workforce is employed by a nonprofit? Nonprofits are integral to the economy, contributing to both the social and financial health of the communities they serve.

Innovation in the Nonprofit Sector

One of the best aspects of nonprofits is their ability to innovate. Because they're focused on solving problems rather than generating profit, nonprofits have the freedom to experiment with new ideas and approaches.

Whether it's finding a new way to deliver healthcare in underserved areas or developing cutting-edge environmental technologies, nonprofits are often at the forefront of social innovation.

Civic Engagement: The Heart of Community

Nonprofits don't just solve problems—they help build stronger, more engaged communities. They provide platforms for people to get involved in causes they care about, whether through volunteering, donating, or advocacy. By engaging people in meaningful ways, nonprofits strengthen the social fabric and promote a sense of shared responsibility for the well-being of others.

Civic engagement is one of the key roles that nonprofits play in society. They give people the opportunity to contribute, to be part of something bigger, and to make a difference.

Wrapping It All Up: Why Nonprofits Matter

In the end, nonprofits are so much more than service providers. They're advocates, innovators, and community builders. They tackle the biggest issues we face—whether through direct services, policy advocacy, or creating new ways to solve problems. Supporting nonprofits—whether by donating, volunteering, or even spreading the word—helps build a world where compassion, justice, and equality are at the forefront.

As we move forward, it's important to recognize the evolving challenges facing the nonprofit sector. Nonprofits need strong, visionary leadership to navigate these complexities and keep making an impact. With the right resources, accountability, and a commitment to innovation, nonprofits can continue to change the world for the better—one mission at a time.

Chapter 2: Nonprofit CEO Positions and Essential Skill Sets

In the nonprofit sector, the role of a CEO is uniquely challenging and demands a distinct set of skills. Unlike their counterparts in the corporate world, nonprofit CEOs are driven not by profits, but by a mission to make a positive impact on society. This mission-oriented leadership requires deep commitment, adaptability, and a comprehensive understanding of both strategic and operational management. The titles "Executive Director" and "President" are often used interchangeably, but they can imply different responsibilities and roles within an organization. Understanding these distinctions and the core competencies required for nonprofit leadership is crucial for anyone aspiring to hold such a position.

The Importance of Titles: Executive Director vs. President

In the nonprofit world, titles such as "Executive Director" and "President" are more than just designations; they reflect the nature of the role and the organization's structure. The title can influence how the leader is perceived both internally and externally, and it can also shape the scope of their responsibilities.

An Executive Director typically serves as the operational leader of the organization. This role involves managing day-to-day activities, ensuring the organization runs smoothly, and executing strategies developed in collaboration with the board of directors. The Executive Director is often deeply involved in the internal workings of the organization, from overseeing staff and managing budgets to ensuring compliance with legal and regulatory standards.

Conversely, a President might focus more on the strategic and visionary aspects of leadership. In some nonprofits, the President is the public face of the organization, responsible for building relationships with key stakeholders, including donors, community leaders, and policymakers. This role often involves setting the strategic direction of the organization and ensuring it aligns with the mission and vision. While the President may also be involved in operational aspects, their primary focus is on broader organizational leadership.

The choice of title is not merely cosmetic; it can impact the effectiveness of leadership by clarifying the expectations and responsibilities associated with the role. Understanding these distinctions is important for anyone aspiring to lead in the nonprofit sector, as it helps align personal strengths with the needs of the organization.

However, it's important to note that nonprofit organizational structures vary widely. Some organizations use titles interchangeably, while others assign specific roles and responsibilities to each title. For instance, in some cases, the board chair might be called the President, or the Executive Director could also serve as a member of the board. These are not hard-and-fast rules but general guidelines. Moving forward, I will refer to this position as the Chief Executive Officer (CEO), acknowledging that both titles represent the top paid position within an organization.

Why Become a Nonprofit CEO?

Aspiring to be a nonprofit CEO is more than just seeking a prestigious title; it requires a deep-rooted commitment to the cause and a desire to lead an organization toward meaningful change. The motivations behind wanting to take on this role should be thoroughly examined because they will drive your actions and decisions during challenging times.

One of the most critical questions to ask yourself is, "Why do I want to be a nonprofit CEO?" This question is not just about career aspirations; it's about understanding your core values and how they align with the organization's mission. Nonprofit leadership is demanding, often requiring long hours, emotional resilience, and the ability to navigate complex challenges. Without a strong, personal connection to the mission, it can be difficult to maintain the energy and commitment needed to lead effectively.

For many, the "why" is rooted in personal experiences or a deep passion for the cause. It might be the desire to make a difference, lead a movement for social change, or contribute to a mission that aligns with personal values. Maybe you had a relative who fought a particular disease, your family received help from a food bank when you were young, or perhaps you want to help more kids graduate from high school. Whatever your motivation, it should be compelling enough to sustain you through the inevitable difficulties of leading a nonprofit organization.

Core Skills for Effective Nonprofit Leadership

Leading a nonprofit organization requires a unique blend of skills that go beyond traditional management. The role of a nonprofit CEO demands a balance between strategic vision, operational acumen, and the ability to inspire and motivate others. While some skills may have helped you reach the leadership position, sustaining and growing in the role requires continuous development and adaptation.

- Visionary Leadership with Operational Focus: Effective nonprofit CEOs are both visionaries and tacticians. They can see the big picture and set a strategic direction for the organization while breaking that vision into actionable steps. This dual focus allows them to drive the organization forward while ensuring that day-to-day operations align with long-term goals.

- Passion and Commitment to the Mission: Passion is the fuel that drives nonprofit leaders. A deep commitment to the organization's mission is essential for sustaining energy and resilience. This passion must be genuine, as it will inspire others and help build a strong, cohesive team dedicated to achieving the organization's goals.

- Emotional Intelligence and Relational Leadership: Nonprofit CEOs must be adept at building and maintaining relationships with a wide range of stakeholders, including board members, staff, volunteers, donors, and community partners. Emotional intelligence is crucial for managing these relationships, as it involves empathy, active listening, and the ability to navigate complex interpersonal dynamics.

- Strategic Financial Management: Financial acumen is critical for nonprofit leaders. CEOs must be able to manage budgets effectively, understand financial statements, and identify both opportunities and risks. They must also be adept at fundraising, understanding the nuances of donor relations, and securing the financial resources needed to sustain and grow the organization.

- Resilience and Adaptability: The nonprofit sector is often unpredictable, with shifting funding landscapes, evolving community needs, and external challenges. Effective CEOs must be resilient and adaptable, capable of navigating uncertainty and leading the organization through change. This includes handling adversity with grace, maintaining focus on the mission, and persevering through difficult times.

- Servant Leadership: Coined by management expert Robert Greenleaf in 1970, servant leadership is particularly relevant in the nonprofit sector. CEOs often prioritize the needs of others, focusing on empowering their team and fostering a collaborative, inclusive culture. This leadership style is essential for building trust and ensuring the organization operates with integrity and transparency.

- Communication and Public Speaking: As the face of the organization, nonprofit CEOs must be effective communicators. This includes public speaking, writing, and interpersonal communication skills. They must be able to articulate the organization's mission and vision compellingly, whether speaking to donors, the media, or the community.

- Strategic Planning and Implementation: Beyond setting a vision, nonprofit CEOs must be skilled at strategic planning and execution. This involves developing long-term plans, setting goals, and implementing strategies that move the organization forward. It also requires the ability to monitor progress, make adjustments, and ensure the organization remains focused on its mission.

Different Leadership Styles in the Nonprofit Sector

Just as there are various titles for nonprofit leaders, there are also different leadership styles that can be effective, depending on the organization's needs and the leader's strengths. Understanding your leadership style and how it aligns with the organization's culture and goals is crucial for success.

- Visionary Leadership: Visionary leaders are focused on the future, often setting ambitious goals and inspiring others to follow. They are innovative, forward-thinking, and skilled at motivating others to embrace change. This style is particularly effective in organizations looking to grow, innovate, or reposition themselves in the sector.

- Operational Leadership: Operational leaders excel at managing day-to-day activities. They are detail-oriented, practical, and focused on efficiency and effectiveness. This leadership style is essential for organizations that require strong internal management to maintain stability and achieve their objectives.

- Servant Leadership: Servant leaders prioritize the needs of their team and the community they serve. They focus on empowering others, fostering collaboration, and creating an inclusive organizational culture. This style is well-suited to nonprofits, where the mission often requires collective effort and shared commitment.

- Transformational Leadership: Transformational leaders are change agents who focus on driving significant organizational change. They are skilled at inspiring others, challenging the status quo, and leading organizations through periods of transformation. This style is ideal for nonprofits facing significant challenges or opportunities for growth.

- Relational Leadership: Relational leaders build strong networks and partnerships. They are adept at connecting with people, building trust, and leveraging relationships to achieve the organization's goals. This style is particularly valuable in nonprofits that rely heavily on collaboration with external stakeholders.

- Analytical Leadership: Analytical leaders are data-driven and focus on evidence-based decision-making. They are skilled at evaluating programs, measuring impact, and using data to guide strategy. This style is important for organizations that prioritize accountability and need to demonstrate their effectiveness to donors and stakeholders.

While each leadership style has its strengths, the most effective nonprofit CEOs are often those who can adapt their style to meet the needs of the organization and its stakeholders. Understanding your leadership style and how it influences your approach to decision-making, communication, and team dynamics is crucial for effective leadership.

Navigating the Complexities of Nonprofit Leadership

Leading a nonprofit organization is a complex and multifaceted role. It requires a balance of visionary thinking, operational expertise, and emotional intelligence. Nonprofit CEOs must navigate challenges ranging from financial management and fundraising to community engagement and strategic planning. They must also be resilient, adaptable, and deeply committed to their organization's mission.

The title you hold—whether CEO, Executive Director, President, or another designation—carries significant responsibility and offers the opportunity to make a meaningful impact. Understanding the skills required for nonprofit leadership and how to develop them is essential for anyone aspiring to lead in this sector.

Ultimately, the role of a nonprofit CEO is both challenging and rewarding. It offers the opportunity to guide an organization toward achieving its mission, inspire and empower others, and make a positive difference in the world. By cultivating the necessary skills, understanding your leadership style, and staying true to your "why," you can navigate the complexities of this role and drive your organization toward success.

Chapter 3: Applying for a Nonprofit CEO Position

The journey to becoming a nonprofit CEO is both exhilarating and challenging. Whether you're considering an internal promotion, eyeing a local nonprofit, or contemplating a move to lead an organization in a different state, the process requires thorough preparation and a deep understanding of the organization you wish to lead. Applying for a nonprofit CEO position isn't just about submitting a resume and attending an interview; it's about demonstrating your alignment with the organization's mission, showcasing your leadership abilities, and proving that you're the right person to take the organization forward. This chapter will guide you through the critical steps in applying for a nonprofit CEO role, ensuring you're well-prepared to make your best case.

You Found the One: Understanding the Organization

Finding the right nonprofit CEO position is often the result of careful consideration and research. Whether you've come across an internal promotion opportunity, a position at a local nonprofit, or a role with an organization in another state, the first step is to truly understand the organization. This involves more than just knowing the job title and location—you need to delve into the organization's core.

Start by examining the organization's mission and vision. These statements are the heart of any nonprofit and should resonate with your personal values and professional goals. Ask yourself: *Does this mission inspire me? Can I see myself dedicating my time and energy to advancing this cause?* If the answer is yes, you're on the right path.

Next, take a close look at the organization's clients and stakeholders. Who does the organization serve? What are the demographics and needs of their client base? Understanding the people and communities the organization supports will help you tailor your application and demonstrate your commitment to their cause.

Equally important is understanding the organization's current focus. Review recent initiatives, programs, and campaigns. What are their priorities? Are they focused on expanding services, increasing advocacy efforts, or improving operational efficiency? Knowing the organization's present objectives will allow you to position yourself as a candidate who is not only aware of their work but also capable of leading it.

Lastly, familiarize yourself with the organization's funding sources. Are they reliant on grants, individual donations, corporate sponsorships, or government contracts? This financial insight is critical, as a major responsibility of the CEO will be ensuring the organization's financial sustainability.

Following the Process: Reading the Job Description Carefully

Once you've decided to apply, the next step is to thoroughly review the job description. This document is more than a list of duties—it's a blueprint of the organization's expectations and priorities for their next leader.

Carefully read the job description and highlight key responsibilities, required skills, and qualifications. These are the areas to focus on in your application. Ask yourself how your experience aligns with these duties and how you can demonstrate that you meet or exceed the qualifications. If the job description emphasizes fundraising, for instance, make sure to highlight your success in securing major gifts or grants. If strategic planning is a key responsibility, provide examples of how you've developed and implemented successful strategies in previous roles.

Additionally, pay attention to recommended skills or experiences that aren't required but are considered valuable. These could be the differentiators that set you apart from other candidates. For example, if the position mentions experience with a specific population or geographic area, be sure to emphasize any relevant background you have.

Remember, the job description is your guide, and your application should reflect a deep understanding of these expectations. Tailor your resume and cover letter to align with the language and priorities in the job description. This not only shows you've done your homework but also positions you as a candidate who is prepared to fulfill the role.

Knowing the Organization's Mission: The Key to Success

One of the most important aspects of applying for a nonprofit CEO position is demonstrating your alignment with the organization's mission. The mission statement is the driving force behind everything the organization does, and as a potential leader, you must show that you're not only familiar with the mission but also deeply committed to advancing it.

Your cover letter is an excellent place to express your passion for the mission. Share any personal connection to the cause, whether through professional experiences, volunteer work, or personal beliefs. Highlight how your values align with the organization's mission and how you envision contributing to its success. This connection is crucial—nonprofit boards are looking for leaders who aren't just skilled managers but also passionate advocates for the cause.

Additionally, be prepared to discuss the mission during the interview process. You may be asked how you would further the mission or how your leadership style aligns with the organization's goals. Having a well-thought-out answer that reflects both your understanding of the mission and your strategic vision for the organization will make a strong impression.

Selling Yourself: Highlighting Your Stories and Successes

When applying for a nonprofit CEO position, it's essential to sell yourself by highlighting your relevant experiences and successes. This is your opportunity to demonstrate that you have the skills and experience to lead the organization effectively.

Start by reflecting on your past experiences in the nonprofit sector or in roles with transferable skills. Have you volunteered for the organization before? If so, discuss how this experience has prepared you for the CEO role. Have you worked for or volunteered with another nonprofit that has a similar mission or structure? Highlight the skills and knowledge you gained and how they apply to the organization you're applying to lead.

If your experience comes from outside the nonprofit sector, focus on the transferable skills that make you a strong candidate. For example, if you've led a successful business, discuss your experience in strategic planning, financial management, and team leadership. Explain how these skills will benefit the nonprofit and help it achieve its goals.

Incorporate stories that illustrate your leadership abilities and successes. Did you lead a successful fundraising campaign that exceeded its goals? Did you turn around an organization or department facing significant challenges? Use these examples to demonstrate your ability to lead, inspire, and achieve results.

When discussing your successes, quantify them whenever possible. For instance, instead of saying you "increased donations," say you "increased donations by

25% over two years, resulting in $500,000 in additional funding." This specificity not only strengthens your case but also shows you understand the importance of measurable outcomes in the nonprofit sector.

Understanding the Size and Scope of the Organization

Before applying for a nonprofit CEO position, it's crucial to understand the size and scope of the organization. This includes knowing the organization's budget, staff size, and volunteer base, as these factors will significantly influence your role as CEO.

Start by researching the organization's budget. Understanding the financial resources available will help you assess its capacity to achieve its mission and sustain operations. Review the organization's Form 990, which provides detailed financial information, including revenue sources, expenses, and assets. This information will give you insight into the organization's financial health and any potential challenges you might face as CEO.

Next, consider the size of the staff and volunteer base. How many employees does the organization have? What are the key roles and departments? Understanding the organizational structure will help you gauge the level of leadership and management required. Additionally, knowing the number of volunteers and their roles can provide insight into the organization's culture and community engagement strategies.

Understanding the size and scope of the organization will not only help you tailor your application but also prepare you for the interview process, where you may be asked about your experience managing teams or budgets of similar size.

Doing Your Homework: Knowing the Key Players

One of the most important steps in preparing to apply for a nonprofit CEO position is researching the key players within the organization. This includes understanding who is on the interview committee, who the current leaders are, and who the influential volunteers and staff members are.

Start by identifying the members of the interview committee. This information might be available in the job posting, or you may need to inquire during the application process. Knowing who will be interviewing you allows you to tailor your responses to their interests and concerns. For example, if the board chair is particularly focused on financial sustainability, be prepared to discuss your experience in financial management and fundraising.

Next, research the current leadership within the organization, including both staff and volunteer leaders. Understanding the leadership team's strengths, priorities, and challenges will help you position yourself as someone who can complement and enhance the existing team. It's also important to be aware of any recent leadership transitions, as these can provide context for the organization's current needs and goals.

Additionally, consider the role of volunteers in the organization. Many nonprofits rely heavily on volunteers, and understanding the dynamics of the volunteer base can offer valuable insights into the organization's culture and community engagement.

Lastly, familiarize yourself with key stakeholders, such as major donors, community partners, or government officials. Understanding who these stakeholders are and what their interests might be can help you demonstrate your ability to build and maintain critical relationships as CEO.

The Role of Search Firms and Online Searches

In today's job market, nonprofit CEO positions are often filled through search firms, online job boards, or internal promotions. Understanding these processes can help you navigate the application process more effectively.

If a search firm is involved, take time to understand their role and the criteria they use to evaluate candidates. Search firms often have deep connections within the nonprofit sector and can provide valuable insights into what the organization is looking for in a leader. If possible, establish a relationship with the search firm, as they can offer guidance on how to position yourself as a top candidate.

Online job boards and nonprofit-specific career websites are also common places to find nonprofit CEO positions. When applying through these platforms, follow the application instructions carefully and ensure that your materials are tailored to the specific role. Generic applications are unlikely to stand out, so take the time to customize your resume and cover letter for each position.

Internal promotions are another common pathway to a nonprofit CEO role. If you are already working within the organization, this can be both an advantage and a challenge. On one hand, you have a deep understanding of the organization and its mission; on the other hand, you may need to demonstrate that you're capable of stepping into a higher leadership role. Emphasize your achievements within the organization and how they have prepared you for the CEO role.

The Path to Nonprofit Leadership

Applying for a nonprofit CEO position is a rigorous process that requires thorough preparation, a deep understanding of the organization, and the ability to effectively sell yourself as the right candidate. By taking the time to research the organization, understand its mission, and align your skills and experiences with the job description, you can position yourself as a strong contender for the role.

Remember, the role of a nonprofit CEO is not just about managing an organization; it's about working closely with staff, board members, and volunteers, leading it toward its mission, and making a positive impact on the community it serves. As you navigate the application process, keep your focus on how you can contribute to the organization's success and be a catalyst for change. With the right preparation and mindset, you can take the first step toward becoming a transformative leader in the nonprofit sector.

Chapter 4: Know Your Organization

Once you're in the seat, serving in a leadership role, understanding the organization you are part of is fundamental to your success as a leader, employee, or volunteer in the nonprofit sector. The depth of your knowledge and belief in the mission, vision, and history of your organization can significantly impact your ability to inspire others, overcome challenges, and drive the organization toward its goals. In this chapter, we'll explore the key elements that make up the foundation of organizational knowledge and why they are critical to your effectiveness within the nonprofit world.

Mission and Vision: The Heartbeat of the Organization

The mission and vision statements of a nonprofit organization are more than just words on a page—they are the guiding principles that shape every decision, action, and strategy. The mission statement articulates the core purpose of the organization, outlining what it seeks to achieve and whom it serves. The vision statement, on the other hand, paints a picture of the future the organization aspires to create. Together, these statements provide clear direction and motivation for everyone involved.

Belief in the mission and vision is essential for anyone working in a nonprofit. If you don't genuinely believe in what the organization stands for, it will be difficult to stay motivated and engaged over the long term. Nonprofit work can be challenging, often requiring long hours, creative problem-solving, and a high level of commitment. Without a deep connection to the organization's mission, you may find yourself burning out or feeling disconnected from the work.

To truly embrace the mission and vision, take time to reflect on how they resonate with your values and passions. Ask yourself why you are drawn to this particular organization and how its goals align with your personal beliefs. When you can articulate this connection, you'll be better equipped to inspire others — whether they are colleagues, volunteers, or donors.

Sharing Your Passion for the Work

Passion is contagious. When you are genuinely enthusiastic about the work your organization does, it shows — and it can be incredibly motivating for those around you. Sharing your passion for the mission is one of the most effective ways to build a strong team, engage supporters, and foster a sense of community within the organization.

Start by being open about why you care about the cause. Share personal stories or experiences that have shaped your commitment to the organization's mission. Whether speaking with a potential donor, a new volunteer, or a longtime colleague, your enthusiasm can help them see the value of the work and feel more connected to the cause.

It's also important to create opportunities for others to share their passion. Encourage open dialogue about what inspires each team member and why they are involved in the organization. By fostering a culture of shared passion, you can strengthen the team's sense of purpose and unity—critical for overcoming challenges and achieving the organization's goals.

Knowing the Organization's History

Every nonprofit has a history, and understanding it is crucial to your success within the organization. The history provides context for where the organization is today and where it is headed. It includes the story of how and why the organization was founded, key milestones and achievements, and the evolution of its mission and programs over time.

If your organization is part of a larger network or has a parent organization, it's important to understand the history of those entities as well. This knowledge can help you see the bigger picture and understand how your organization fits into the broader landscape of the nonprofit sector. It also provides insight into the values and traditions that have shaped the organization's culture.

In addition to knowing the positive aspects of the organization's history, it's important to be aware of any past mistakes or scandals. No organization is perfect, and there may have been times when it faced criticism, legal challenges, or internal conflict. Understanding these events and how the organization has learned from them is crucial for building trust with stakeholders and avoiding similar pitfalls in the future.

When discussing the organization's history, be honest about both the successes and challenges. Transparency is key to maintaining credibility and fostering a culture of continuous improvement. By acknowledging past mistakes and demonstrating how the organization has grown from them, you can build a stronger foundation for future success.

Understanding the Organization's Role in the Community

Nonprofits exist to serve communities, whether local, national, or global. Understanding the specific community or communities your organization works with is essential to leading effectively. This involves more than just knowing the demographics or geographic area—it means understanding the needs, challenges, and dynamics of the community, as well as how your organization fits into the broader ecosystem of service providers and stakeholders.

Start by getting to know the community on a personal level. Attend community events, engage with local leaders, and listen to the people your organization serves. This direct engagement will provide valuable insights into the community's needs and how your organization can best meet them. It will also help you build relationships and trust within the community, which is critical for long-term success.

Understanding the organization's role in the community also means recognizing its strengths and limitations. No single organization can solve all of a community's problems, and it's important to be realistic about what your organization can achieve. Collaborating with other nonprofits, government agencies, businesses, and community groups can help you leverage resources and expertise to have a greater impact.

Lastly, be mindful of how your organization's work is perceived in the community. Are there any misconceptions or concerns that need to be addressed? How can you improve communication and transparency to build stronger relationships with community members? By actively engaging with the community and being responsive to its needs, you can ensure that your organization remains relevant and effective in its mission.

Learning from Past Mistakes or Scandals

As mentioned earlier, every organization has faced challenges or made mistakes at some point in its history. How the organization responds to these situations can have a lasting impact on its reputation and effectiveness. It's important to learn from these experiences and use them as opportunities for growth and improvement.

If your organization has been involved in a scandal or controversy, it's essential to understand the details and the steps taken to address the issue. This includes knowing the facts, key players involved, and outcomes of any investigations or corrective actions. Understanding these events helps you avoid repeating the same mistakes and equips you to speak knowledgeably if the issue arises with stakeholders.

In addition to understanding past mistakes, consider how the organization has implemented changes to prevent similar issues in the future. This might involve new policies, governance structures, or training programs designed to address the root causes of the problem. By demonstrating a commitment to learning and improvement, your organization can rebuild trust and strengthen its foundation for the future.

The Power of Knowing Your Organization

Knowing your organization inside and out is not just about being informed—it's about being empowered to lead with confidence, inspire others, and make meaningful contributions to the organization's mission. By understanding the mission and vision, sharing your passion for the work, knowing the organization's history, understanding its role in the community, and learning from past mistakes, you can build a strong foundation for success.

In the nonprofit sector, where the stakes are high and challenges numerous, this deep knowledge and commitment are essential. When you know your organization well, you're better equipped to navigate obstacles, build strong relationships, and drive the organization toward its goals. Ultimately, this knowledge enables you to make a greater impact and help your organization achieve its mission of making the world a better place.

Chapter 5: The Importance of Relationships

In the world of nonprofit leadership, relationships are everything. As a CEO, your ability to build, nurture, and maintain strong relationships with staff, board members, donors, volunteers, and the community is critical to your success and the success of your organization. While your title may give you authority, it's your relationships that will enable you to lead effectively, drive your organization's mission forward, and navigate the inevitable challenges that come with the role.

The Foundation of Leadership: Building Relationships

Being a nonprofit CEO is more than just holding a title or being the boss—it's about being a leader who inspires, motivates, and connects with others. Leadership in the nonprofit sector requires a unique blend of vision, empathy, and collaboration. While you are responsible for ensuring that your organization fulfills its mission, hires the right people, and secures necessary funding, you cannot do it all alone. The most successful nonprofit leaders understand that they must work closely with their board, staff, volunteers, donors, and the broader community to achieve their goals.

Building strong relationships with key stakeholders is not just a nice-to-have—it's essential to your ability to lead effectively. When your team is aligned, motivated, and committed to the mission, remarkable things can be achieved. Conversely, if relationships are strained or neglected, it can lead to discord, inefficiency, and even organizational failure.

As CEO, you set the tone for the organization's culture and the way relationships are managed. Leadership is not about exerting power or control—it's about collaboration and partnership. Your role is to bring people together, foster a sense of shared purpose, and ensure that everyone is working toward the same goals. If you're moving forward without your team behind you, you're not leading—you're just wandering around.

Relationships with Your Staff: Leading with Empathy and Respect

Your relationship with your staff is one of the most important aspects of your role as a nonprofit CEO. Your staff members carry out the day-to-day work of the organization, and their commitment, motivation, and satisfaction are directly tied to your ability to lead effectively.

To build strong relationships with your staff, you must lead with empathy and respect. This means listening to their concerns, valuing their input, and creating an environment where they feel supported and empowered. It also means being transparent and honest in your communications, especially when dealing with difficult decisions or organizational challenges.

One of the most effective ways to build trust with your staff is to be present and accessible. Engage with your team regularly—whether through one-on-one meetings, team check-ins, or informal conversations. Show genuine interest in their work, celebrate their successes, and provide constructive feedback when needed. By fostering a culture of open communication and mutual respect, you'll create a strong foundation for collaboration and teamwork.

It's also important to recognize that as CEO, you are responsible for making tough decisions, including hiring and firing staff when necessary. While these decisions are never easy, they are crucial for maintaining the health and effectiveness of the organization. When making such decisions, handle them with care and compassion, considering the impact on both individuals and the organization as a whole.

Relationships with Your Board: Partnering for Success

Your relationship with your board of directors is another critical aspect of your role as a nonprofit CEO. The board is responsible for governance, oversight, and strategic direction, and your ability to work effectively with them will have a significant impact on your success.

Building a strong partnership with your board starts with understanding their role and responsibilities. While the board is there to support you, they also have a duty to hold you accountable and ensure that the organization is fulfilling its mission. To foster a productive relationship, establish clear expectations and open lines of communication.

One key to a successful CEO-board relationship is transparency. Keep your board informed about the organization's progress, challenges, and opportunities. Share both successes and setbacks, and seek their input and advice when needed. Transparency builds trust and ensures the board remains engaged and invested in the organization's success.

Recognize that board members bring valuable skills, experience, and connections to the table. Take time to get to know each member individually, understand their strengths, and find ways to leverage their expertise for the organization's benefit. Encourage board members to play an active role in fundraising, advocacy, and strategic planning, and show appreciation for their contributions.

Finally, remember that board members are volunteers who are passionate about the organization's mission. Building strong relationships with your board will help you navigate challenges and ensure that the board remains committed and engaged over the long term.

Relationships with Donors: The Art of Fundraising

Fundraising is a central part of your job as a nonprofit CEO, and at the heart of successful fundraising is the ability to build and maintain strong relationships with donors. Donors are not just sources of financial support—they are partners in your mission. Your ability to connect with them on a personal level, build trust, and demonstrate the impact of their contributions will determine the success of your fundraising efforts.

Building relationships with donors starts with understanding their motivations. Why do they support your organization? What are their philanthropic goals? What are their expectations for involvement? By taking the time to get to know your donors and understand their interests, you can tailor your approach and ensure they feel valued and appreciated.

Communication is key to building strong donor relationships. Keep donors informed about the impact of their contributions, share stories of success, and show them how their support is making a difference. Regular updates on the organization's progress and invitations to events and activities can help donors see the mission in action.

Fundraising is not just about asking for money—it's about building trust and relationships. Be genuine in your interactions, and focus on building long-term partnerships rather than just securing one-time gifts. When donors feel connected to the organization and believe in its mission, they are more likely to continue their support and even increase contributions over time.

Relationships with Volunteers: Fostering a Culture of Engagement

Volunteers are the lifeblood of many nonprofit organizations. They give their time, energy, and expertise to support the mission, and your ability to build strong relationships with them is crucial to your success as a nonprofit CEO.

Building relationships with volunteers starts with creating a welcoming and inclusive environment. Make sure volunteers feel valued and appreciated from the moment they join. Provide clear expectations, training, and support so they feel confident and capable in their roles.

Volunteers come from diverse backgrounds and have different motivations for getting involved. Some may be passionate about the mission, while others are looking to give back or gain new skills. Take time to get to know your volunteers and understand their goals and interests. This will help you match them with the right opportunities and keep them engaged long-term.

Communication is key to building strong volunteer relationships. Keep them informed about the organization's activities, progress, and needs, and provide regular opportunities for feedback. Recognize their contributions and celebrate their successes, whether through formal recognition programs or informal gestures of appreciation.

By fostering a culture of engagement and appreciation, you'll build a strong and committed volunteer base motivated to support the organization's mission.

Relationships with the Community: Being a Leader and a Partner

As a nonprofit CEO, your relationship with the broader community is crucial to your organization's success. The community is not only the beneficiary of your organization's work but also a key partner in achieving your mission. Building strong relationships with community members, leaders, and organizations will help you create a network of support and collaboration that amplifies your impact.

To build strong community relationships, start by being an active and visible presence. Attend local events, participate in community meetings, and engage with community leaders. Show that your organization is committed to the community's well-being and that you are listening to their needs and concerns.

Collaboration is essential to building community relationships. Seek partnerships with other organizations, businesses, and government agencies that share your mission or serve the same population. By working together, you can leverage resources, share expertise, and achieve greater impact.

Communication is also key. Keep the community informed about your organization's work and impact, and be transparent about your goals and challenges. Invite community members to get involved—whether through volunteering, attending events, or supporting your efforts.

By building strong community relationships, you'll create a network of support that helps your organization achieve its mission and make a lasting impact.

The Warning: Dealing with Bullies and Mean Girls

Unfortunately, not all relationships are positive. As a nonprofit CEO, you may encounter individuals who are difficult, disruptive, or even toxic. These "bullies" or "mean girls" can create a negative atmosphere, undermine your leadership, and harm the organization's culture.

Dealing with difficult individuals is never easy, but it's important to address these issues head-on. Start by setting clear expectations for behavior and communication within the organization. Make it clear that bullying, harassment, or any form of toxic behavior will not be tolerated.

If you encounter a difficult individual, approach the situation with empathy and professionalism. Try to understand their perspective and address their concerns constructively. However, if the behavior continues or escalates, be prepared to take decisive action—whether it involves mediating conflicts, setting boundaries, or removing individuals from their roles.

Protect yourself and the organization from the negative impact of toxic individuals. Surround yourself with a strong support system, including trusted staff, board members, and mentors. Seek advice when needed, and don't hesitate to take action to protect the organization's culture and mission.

Relationships Are the Heart of Nonprofit Leadership

In the end, relationships are the heart of nonprofit leadership. As a CEO, your ability to build and maintain strong relationships with your staff, board, donors, volunteers, and the community will determine your success and the success of your organization. By leading with empathy, respect, and collaboration, you can create a positive and supportive environment where everyone is working together to achieve the organization's mission.

Remember, being a nonprofit CEO is not just about holding a title or being in charge—it's about being a leader who inspires and connects with others. By building strong relationships, you'll not only achieve your organization's goals but also make a lasting impact on the community you serve.

Chapter 6: Understanding Your Board

As a new nonprofit CEO, one of your most critical relationships will be with your board of directors. This group of individuals, often volunteers from the community or the organization's service area, plays a pivotal role in the success of your organization. For many new CEOs, working closely with a board may be a novel experience, and understanding the dynamics, responsibilities, and expectations of this relationship is essential to your success in the role.

The board of directors is not just another group of stakeholders—they are, in many ways, your new boss. While donors, clients, and staff are all vital to the organization, the board holds ultimate authority over the direction and governance of the nonprofit. Their primary duties include hiring and reviewing the CEO, setting strategic goals in collaboration with the CEO, and, if necessary, making the difficult decision to terminate the CEO's employment. Therefore, the role of a nonprofit CEO revolves around maintaining a strong, transparent, and collaborative relationship with the board.

This chapter will guide you through understanding who your board members are, how to communicate effectively with them, the importance of committees, and how to recruit and manage board members to create a diverse, equitable, and inclusive governance structure.

Who Are Your Board Members?

The first step in building a strong relationship with your board is understanding who your board members are. Board members typically come from diverse backgrounds and bring a variety of skills, experiences, and perspectives to the table. They are usually volunteers with a passion for the organization's mission and a commitment to its success.

Get to Know Your Board Chair

One of the most important relationships you will have as a nonprofit CEO is with your board chair. The board chair is often seen as the leader of the board and serves as the primary point of contact between the board and the CEO. This individual plays a crucial role in setting the tone for board meetings, guiding discussions, and ensuring the board fulfills its responsibilities.

Getting to know your board chair on both a personal and professional level is essential. Schedule regular meetings to discuss the organization's progress, challenges, and opportunities. These meetings should be open and honest, allowing both of you to share your thoughts and concerns. The board chair can be a valuable sounding board for ideas and a source of support when navigating difficult situations.

Building a strong relationship with your board chair requires mutual respect and trust. They should feel confident in your ability to lead, and you should feel supported in your role. Fostering this relationship can create a partnership that benefits the entire organization.

Understanding the Bylaws and the Board's Role

Every nonprofit operates under a set of bylaws—legal documents that outline the governance structure, roles, and responsibilities of the board and its members. As a new CEO, it is crucial to familiarize yourself with these bylaws. They will provide you with a clear understanding of how the board functions, the process for electing or appointing board members, the terms of service, and the specific duties of the board.

The bylaws will also define the relationship between the board and the CEO. Understanding these guidelines will help you navigate the complex dynamics of board governance and ensure that you are fulfilling your responsibilities within the framework established by the organization.

In addition to the bylaws, take the time to learn about the history and culture of the board. How has the board evolved over time? What are its traditions and norms? Understanding the board's history and culture provides valuable context as you build relationships with its members.

The Four Most Common Types of Nonprofit Boards

As a nonprofit CEO, understanding the different types of boards and how they function is crucial for ensuring your organization runs smoothly. Each type of board plays a unique role, and knowing how to work with them effectively can greatly influence the success of your nonprofit. Here, we explore four common types of nonprofit boards: the Governance Board, Advisory Board, Fundraising Board, and Working Board.

Governance Board

The Governance Board is the most traditional and formal type of board for nonprofits. Its primary responsibility is to provide oversight, ensuring that the organization adheres to its mission, follows legal requirements, and maintains financial stability. Members of a Governance Board are responsible for high-level decision-making, strategic planning, and ensuring the nonprofit's long-term sustainability. They also have fiduciary responsibilities, meaning they must act in the organization's best interest and ensure it remains financially sound.

Governance Board members typically bring diverse skills in areas such as finance, legal, human resources, and marketing. These members work closely with the CEO to set goals, evaluate performance, and make strategic decisions. While Governance Board members may not be involved in day-to-day operations, their oversight is critical to the nonprofit's success and longevity. As a CEO, maintaining open, transparent communication with your Governance Board ensures that leadership and the board are aligned.

Advisory Board

An Advisory Board serves as a valuable resource, offering expertise, advice, and support to the organization without the formal responsibilities of governance. Unlike a Board of Directors, an Advisory Board does not have legal or fiduciary duties and is not involved in management or decision-making. Instead, they act as a think tank, offering insights and recommendations on key initiatives, strategies, or specific areas where the organization needs additional expertise.

An Advisory Board might include professionals in law, finance, marketing, or subject matter experts relevant to the nonprofit's mission. Their role is to advise, not to govern, so they aren't accountable for the organization's success or failure. As a CEO, working with an Advisory Board can provide critical insights to help shape your organization's strategy and enhance decision-making.

Fundraising Board

A Fundraising Board, as the name suggests, focuses primarily on generating financial support for the organization. This type of board is often composed of individuals with significant connections within the community or industry, and they are willing to leverage their networks to raise funds for the nonprofit. Members of a Fundraising Board may host or sponsor events, connect the organization with potential major donors, or assist in developing a comprehensive fundraising strategy.

Fundraising Board members are usually expected to contribute financially to the organization themselves, setting an example for others. They may also be tasked with finding corporate sponsorships or encouraging their networks to donate or attend fundraising events. As a CEO, collaborating with a Fundraising Board can significantly enhance your organization's fundraising efforts and help secure the resources needed to fulfill your mission.

Working Board

A Working Board is most common in smaller or newer nonprofits that may not yet have the budget for a large staff. In this model, board members take on active roles in day-to-day operations, helping carry out essential functions needed to run the organization. This can include anything from organizing events to managing finances, creating marketing materials, or even helping with administrative tasks.

While the Working Board maintains governance responsibilities, its members are hands-on, often working alongside staff and volunteers to execute the organization's programs and services. As a CEO, you will work closely with a Working Board, relying on its members for both strategic oversight and practical support. This type of board can be highly effective when financial resources are limited, but as the organization grows, the goal is often to transition to a more traditional Governance Board.

Communicate Clearly and Often

Effective communication is the cornerstone of a successful relationship between a nonprofit CEO and the board. As CEO, you are responsible for keeping the board informed about all aspects of the organization, from day-to-day operations to long-term strategic goals. Communication should be clear, consistent, and transparent.

Never Let the Board Be Caught Off Guard

One cardinal rule of nonprofit leadership is never to let your board be caught off guard—whether by good news or bad. Surprising the board with unexpected developments can erode trust and lead to unnecessary tension. Instead, strive to keep the board informed in real time, especially regarding significant events or challenges.

Provide regular updates to the board through various channels, such as monthly or quarterly reports, email updates, and regular board meetings. Highlight both successes and challenges, and provide context for any issues. By being proactive in your communication, you ensure that the board is always in the loop and prepared to support the organization when needed.

In times of crisis or when facing difficult decisions, prompt and thorough communication is especially important. Whether dealing with a financial shortfall, public relations issue, or internal conflict, inform the board as soon as possible. Present the situation clearly, outline the potential impact, and provide recommendations for moving forward. Transparency builds trust and demonstrates your commitment to the organization's success.

Sharing Information with Committees

Board committees are an integral part of nonprofit governance, focusing on specific areas such as finance, fundraising, governance, and programs. As CEO, it is important to share relevant information with committees and engage them in the organization's work.

Committees can serve as some of the best ambassadors for your organization. Involving them in decision-making processes and leveraging their expertise enhances organizational effectiveness and strengthens relationships with individual board members.

When sharing information with committees, provide them with the data and context they need to make informed decisions. This might include financial reports, program evaluations, or updates on strategic initiatives. Regular communication with committees keeps them engaged and empowers them to actively support the organization.

Recruiting for Time, Treasure, and Talent

Recruiting and retaining effective board members is one of the most important responsibilities of a nonprofit CEO. A strong board brings together individuals with time, treasure, and talent to contribute to the organization's success.

Time

Time is one of the most valuable resources a board member can offer. Board members should be willing and able to dedicate the time necessary to fulfill their responsibilities, including attending meetings, participating in committee work, and engaging in fundraising and advocacy efforts. When recruiting new board members, be clear about the time commitment required and seek individuals who can make that commitment.

Assess the current level of engagement among your board members and identify any gaps in participation. If certain members struggle to meet their commitments, consider having a candid conversation about their ability to continue serving. It's better to have a smaller, fully engaged board than a larger one with limited participation.

Treasure

Treasure refers to the financial resources board members can bring to the organization. While not every member needs to be a major donor, it's important to have individuals willing and able to contribute financially. Board members should also actively participate in fundraising efforts, leveraging their networks to secure donations and support.

When recruiting board members, consider their ability to contribute financially and their willingness to participate in fundraising. Wealth isn't the only consideration—what's most important is their commitment to the organization's financial health.

Talent

Talent encompasses the skills, expertise, and experience board members bring. A well-rounded board includes individuals with diverse backgrounds in finance, marketing, law, nonprofit management, and community relations. These skills are critical for providing effective oversight and strategic guidance.

When recruiting new board members, consider the organization's needs and the skills currently underrepresented on the board. For example, if your organization is planning a capital campaign, it may be beneficial to recruit someone with fundraising or financial planning experience.

Diversity, Equity, and Inclusion in Board Recruitment

In recent years, diversity, equity, and inclusion (DEI) have become increasingly important in nonprofit governance. A diverse board reflects the community it serves and brings a range of perspectives to the table, ensuring decisions are inclusive and equitable.

Prioritize DEI in your board recruitment efforts by actively seeking out members from diverse backgrounds, including different races, ethnicities, genders, ages, sexual orientations, and socioeconomic statuses. Create an inclusive environment where all board members feel valued and heard.

Start by assessing your board's current composition. Are any groups underrepresented? If so, consider partnering with community organizations or using targeted outreach strategies to recruit individuals from those groups. Additionally, consider barriers preventing individuals from serving—offering flexibility in financial expectations or opportunities for in-kind contributions can be helpful.

Retention and engagement are key to maintaining a diverse and inclusive board. Ensure all members have equal opportunities to contribute and that their voices are heard.

The Board as Your New Boss

One of the most important things for a new nonprofit CEO to understand is that the board is, in many ways, your new boss. Nonprofit CEOs are accountable to the board of directors, whose responsibilities include hiring and reviewing the CEO, setting strategic direction, and ensuring the organization fulfills its mission.

Recognize that the board-CEO relationship is a partnership. While the board provides oversight and guidance, the CEO leads the organization day-to-day. Maintaining a strong, collaborative relationship with the board is essential for success.

Start by establishing clear expectations with the board —understand their priorities, how they define success, and their expectations for communication and reporting. By aligning your work with their goals, you ensure that you're meeting their needs.

Transparency and honesty are critical. If you're facing challenges or setbacks, bring them to the board's attention and seek their input on how to address them. Being open builds trust and strengthens the partnership.

Using the Board to Support the Organization

Your board members are some of the best ambassadors for your organization. They are passionate about the mission, well-connected in the community, and bring valuable skills and expertise. As CEO, it's important to leverage these assets to support the organization.

Encourage board members to take active roles in fundraising, advocacy, and community engagement. Provide them with the tools they need, such as talking points, success stories, and impact data. Recognize and celebrate their contributions, and offer opportunities for leadership roles within the board.

Committees are also valuable for supporting the organization. By delegating specific tasks to committees, you can leverage board members' expertise while freeing up time for other important work.

Navigating Your New Relationship with the Board

As a new nonprofit CEO, understanding and building strong relationships with your board is crucial. The board is not just a group of volunteers—they are your partners, advisors, and new bosses. By getting to know your board members, communicating clearly and often, and leveraging their skills and expertise, you can build a strong, collaborative relationship that supports the organization's success.

Remember, the board-CEO relationship is a partnership. Working together, you can achieve great things for your organization and the community it serves. By following these principles, you'll build a successful and fulfilling partnership with your board.

Chapter 7: Meetings and Agendas – Your New Best Friend

As a new nonprofit CEO, meetings will become an integral part of your daily routine. Whether gathering with your board of directors, your staff, or your volunteers, meetings are a critical tool for sharing ideas, making decisions, and driving the organization's mission forward. However, not all meetings are created equal. When poorly managed, they can quickly turn into time-wasting coffee clubs, leaving participants frustrated and disengaged. On the other hand, well-structured meetings with clear agendas can be powerful platforms for collaboration, innovation, and progress.

This chapter will explore the importance of meetings and agendas, how to make them productive, and how to ensure that every meeting serves a clear purpose and achieves its goals.

Meetings with Purpose: Avoiding the Coffee Club Trap

We've all been there—sitting in a meeting that feels like a waste of time, wondering why we're not doing something more productive. Maybe the discussion has veered off-topic, or perhaps there was no clear agenda to guide the conversation in the first place. These "coffee club" meetings, where participants sit around drinking a cup of coffee, seem more focused on chatting and socializing than on getting things done. This is a common pitfall in many organizations.

As a nonprofit CEO, your time and the time of your team are valuable resources that should be used wisely. This means every meeting you hold must have a clear purpose. Before scheduling a meeting, ask yourself: *What is the objective of this meeting? What do I hope to achieve by bringing these people together?* If you can't answer these questions, it's worth reconsidering whether a meeting is necessary at all.

Meetings should be focused on specific topics that require discussion, decision-making, or collaboration. They should not be used as a substitute for simple information sharing, which can often be accomplished more efficiently through email or other communication channels. By ensuring every meeting has a clear purpose, you can avoid the coffee club trap and make the most of your time together.

The Power of a Well-Prepared Agenda

A well-prepared agenda is the cornerstone of a successful meeting. It serves as a roadmap, guiding the conversation and keeping participants focused on key issues. Without an agenda, meetings can easily become disorganized and unproductive, with participants leaving unsure of what was accomplished or what the next steps are.

As a nonprofit CEO, it's your responsibility to ensure that every meeting you hold has a clear, concise agenda that is shared with participants in advance. This allows everyone to come prepared, with a solid understanding of what will be discussed and what is expected of them.

An effective agenda should include the following elements:

- Specific Topics and Items to Discuss: Clearly outline the topics that will be covered during the meeting. These should be specific and actionable rather than vague or broad. For example, instead of listing "Fundraising," specify "Reviewing strategies for the upcoming annual gala" or "Identifying potential corporate sponsors for the next quarter."

- Accountability and Follow-Up: For each item on the agenda, identify who is responsible for leading the discussion, making decisions, or taking action. This creates accountability and ensures that everyone knows their role in the meeting. Additionally, include any necessary follow-up actions and who will be responsible for them. For example, "Andrew will draft the sponsorship letter by next Tuesday" or "Sara will update the project timeline by the end of the week."

- Time Allocation: Assign a specific amount of time to each agenda item. This helps keep the meeting on track and ensures all important topics are covered. Be realistic about how much time each discussion will take, and stick to the schedule as closely as possible.

- Meeting Objective: Begin the agenda with a clear statement of the meeting's objective. This sets the tone for the discussion and reminds everyone of the meeting's purpose.

Sharing the agenda in advance is crucial. Distribute it at least 24 hours before the meeting so participants have time to review it, gather necessary information, and prepare their contributions. This preparation leads to more informed and productive discussions, as everyone arrives ready to engage with the topics at hand.

Staying on Time and On Task

Time management is a critical aspect of running effective meetings. Few things frustrate participants more than a meeting that drags on longer than expected, especially if they have other commitments or tasks to attend to. As CEO, it's your job to respect everyone's time by keeping the meeting on schedule and ensuring that discussions stay on task.

Start the meeting on time, even if some participants are running late. This sets a precedent that meeting time is important and encourages punctuality. If necessary, you can briefly recap for latecomers, but don't let their tardiness delay the start of the meeting.

During the meeting, keep an eye on the clock and gently steer discussions back on track if they begin to drift off-topic. If a particular topic requires more time than anticipated, you may need to adjust the agenda—

either by shortening other discussions or scheduling a follow-up meeting to address unresolved issues.

If the meeting is running behind schedule, communicate this to the participants and get their input on how to proceed. For example, you might say, "We're running 10 minutes behind schedule. Should we extend the meeting by 10 minutes, or would you prefer to schedule another time to finish our discussion on this topic?" This shows respect for their time while ensuring important issues are fully addressed.

Follow-Up: Ensuring Accountability and Progress

The work doesn't end when the meeting is over. What happens after the meeting is just as important as the meeting itself. Follow-up is essential to ensure that decisions made during the meeting are implemented and that progress is made on action items.

After the meeting, send a follow-up email or memo summarizing the key points discussed, decisions made, and actions that need to be taken. Include deadlines for each action item and the names of the individuals responsible. This written record serves as a reference for everyone involved and ensures there is no confusion about what was agreed upon.

Most organizations require minutes for all board meetings, and some require minutes at committee meetings as well. Make sure there is a designated person to take minutes and that they are shared promptly. Many times, especially with small organizations, the CEO may be responsible for the minutes.

It's also important to follow up with individuals assigned tasks or responsibilities. Check in with them periodically to see how they are progressing and offer any support they might need. This not only ensures tasks are completed but also reinforces a culture of accountability within the organization.

Consider including a brief review of the previous meeting's action items at the beginning of your next meeting. This helps keep everyone on track and ensures that no tasks fall through the cracks.

Meetings as a Tool for Building Organizational Momentum

When done well, meetings are not just about getting things done—they are an opportunity to build momentum and excitement within your organization. Meetings can be a platform for sharing success stories, celebrating achievements, and aligning your team around a common purpose.

As a nonprofit CEO, use meetings to reinforce the organization's mission and values. Start each meeting with a brief reminder of the organization's goals or a success story that highlights the impact of your work. This sets a positive tone for the meeting and reminds everyone why they are there.

Encourage participation and collaboration during meetings. Create an environment where everyone feels comfortable sharing ideas and opinions, and make it clear that all contributions are valued. This leads to better decision-making and fosters a sense of ownership and commitment among your team.

Be mindful of the energy in the room. If a meeting is dragging or participants seem disengaged, consider incorporating elements that re-energize the group. This might include taking a short break, incorporating a brainstorming session, or simply acknowledging everyone's hard work.

Avoiding Common Pitfalls: No More Time-Wasting Meetings

One of the most common complaints about meetings is that they are a waste of time. As a nonprofit CEO, it's your job to ensure that this is never the case. By following the principles outlined in this chapter, you can avoid the most common pitfalls of meetings and make them a valuable tool for driving your organization forward.

Here are a few additional tips to avoid time-wasting meetings:

- Be Selective About Attendees: Only invite those who are necessary for the discussion. Including too many people can lead to distractions and make it harder to reach decisions. If certain individuals only need to be informed of the outcomes, consider sharing the meeting summary with them afterward rather than having them attend the entire meeting.

- Don't Over-Schedule Meetings: Avoid the temptation to schedule meetings for every issue that arises. If a discussion can be handled via email, a phone call, or a brief check-in, consider those alternatives instead. Reserve meetings for issues that require group discussion or decision-making.

- Evaluate the Effectiveness of Your Meetings: Periodically assess whether your meetings are achieving their goals. Ask for feedback from participants and be open to making changes to the format, frequency, or structure of your meetings if needed.

- End with Clarity: Always conclude meetings with a clear summary of what was discussed, the decisions made, and the next steps. Ensure everyone knows their responsibilities and deadlines before they leave the room.

Embracing Meetings and Agendas as Strategic Tools

As a new nonprofit CEO, mastering the art of effective meetings and agendas is crucial to your success. By meeting with purpose, preparing thoughtful agendas, managing time effectively, and following up diligently, you can transform meetings from time-wasters into powerful tools for collaboration, decision-making, and momentum building.

Remember, meetings are not just about getting things done—they are about bringing people together to achieve a common goal. By approaching them with intention and structure, you can ensure that every meeting is a step forward for your organization and its mission. Embrace meetings and agendas as your new best friends, and they will serve you well in your leadership journey.

Chapter 8: Know Your Numbers: Budgets and Financials

As a new nonprofit CEO, one of the most critical aspects of your role will be understanding and managing your organization's finances. This includes not only knowing your budget inside and out but also having a clear grasp of your organization's financial statements, tax forms, and overall financial health. While you may have a finance director or department to assist you, the ultimate responsibility for ensuring that your organization remains financially sound rests with you.

This chapter will explore the importance of knowing your numbers, understanding your budget, and how to effectively manage your organization's finances. We'll also discuss the significance of the IRS Form 990, the annual tax return that most nonprofits must file, and why it's crucial for you to be familiar with this document.

Knowing Your Numbers: The Foundation of Financial Leadership

As the CEO of a nonprofit organization, you are responsible for ensuring that your organization stays within its budget and does not spend more money than it can raise or generate. This responsibility is foundational to your role, as financial mismanagement can quickly lead to serious consequences, including loss of donor trust, financial insolvency, and even the closure of the organization.

To be an effective financial leader, you need to know your numbers. This means understanding every aspect of your organization's budget—from how much each program costs to run, to what your monthly payroll is, to how much you pay for rent and utilities. These are questions you should be able to answer off the top of your head because they are essential to making informed decisions about the organization's operations.

Even if you have a finance director or department, it's essential that you, as the CEO, have a thorough understanding of where all the money is being spent and what your organization's income streams are. This knowledge will enable you to make strategic decisions, respond quickly to financial challenges, and communicate effectively with your board, donors, and other stakeholders.

To start, familiarize yourself with your organization's budget. Review each line item and understand what it represents. Ask questions if anything is unclear. How much is allocated for each program? What are the fixed costs, such as rent, salaries, and utilities? What are the variable costs, and how do they fluctuate throughout the year? Understanding these details will give you a clear picture of your organization's financial position and help you identify areas where adjustments may be necessary.

Engaging with Your Board on Financial Matters

Your board of directors plays a crucial role in overseeing the financial health of the organization. As the CEO, it's important to engage the board in discussions about the budget. The board may have a longer history with the organization and can provide valuable context about why certain financial decisions were made in the past. They may also have specific expectations regarding how the budget should be presented and how they want to be involved in financial oversight.

Start by having an open conversation with your board about the organization's financial situation. Share your observations about the budget, including any concerns or areas where you see opportunities for improvement. Encourage board members to ask questions and provide input. This collaborative approach will build trust and ensure that the board is fully informed and engaged in the organization's financial management.

It's also important to understand the board's role in approving the budget. In many nonprofits, the board is responsible for reviewing and approving the annual budget, and they may have specific criteria or expectations that you need to meet. Be prepared to present the budget in a clear, concise manner, and provide supporting documentation that explains the rationale behind the budget allocations.

Additionally, keep the board informed throughout the year about the organization's financial performance. Provide regular updates on how the organization is tracking against the budget, and be transparent about any challenges or unexpected expenses that arise. This ongoing communication ensures that the board remains engaged and supportive of your efforts to manage the organization's finances.

Budgeting for the Unexpected: Planning for Contingencies

One of the most important aspects of creating a budget is planning for the unexpected. While it's impossible to predict every challenge that may arise during the year, it's essential to build flexibility into your budget and be prepared for potential disruptions.

When creating the annual budget, take a walk through the upcoming year and consider factors that could impact your organization's finances. Will there be a loss of major donors? Are your programs and services expected to grow, requiring additional resources? Do you anticipate needing to repair or replace any buildings, vehicles, or equipment that the organization owns? These are all questions that should be considered when preparing the budget.

If you know that it won't be a typical fiscal year—for example, if you're planning a major capital campaign or if the organization is facing significant challenges—make adjustments to the budget to account for these one-offs. This might include setting aside a contingency fund or reallocating resources to address potential risks.

It's also important to be realistic about your revenue projections. While it's natural to be optimistic about fundraising and income, base your budget on realistic assumptions. Consider the worst-case scenario and ensure that the organization has enough financial reserves to weather any unexpected challenges.

By budgeting for the unexpected and planning for contingencies, you help ensure that your organization remains financially stable, even in the face of unforeseen challenges.

Collaborating with Staff on Budget Preparation

One of the best pieces of advice for new nonprofit CEOs is to go directly to the source when calculating the budget. This means collaborating with staff members who are responsible for the organization's programs, services, and operations.

For example, if you want to know how much a particular program costs to run, talk to the program director. They will have the most accurate and up-to-date information about the program's expenses and resource needs. If you need to find out about insurance costs, go directly to your insurance agent and ask for a detailed breakdown of premiums, deductibles, and coverage options.

By involving your staff in the budget preparation process, you ensure the budget is based on real numbers and accurate information. This collaborative approach also helps build buy-in and ownership among staff members, as they see that their input is valued and that they have a role in shaping the organization's financial strategy.

Working closely with staff on budget preparation can also help identify potential efficiencies or cost-saving opportunities. For instance, a program director might suggest ways to streamline operations or reduce expenses without compromising the quality of services. These insights can be invaluable in creating a budget that is both realistic and sustainable.

Understanding the IRS Form 990: The Nonprofit's Financial Report Card

The IRS Form 990 is an essential document for nonprofit organizations. It serves as the annual tax return that most nonprofits must file with the Internal Revenue Service (IRS), and it provides a detailed overview of the organization's finances, governance, and operations. As a nonprofit CEO, it's crucial that you understand what is on your organization's Form 990 and how it reflects your financial management.

The Form 990 is a public document, meaning donors, funders, regulators, and the general public can access it. This transparency is a key aspect of nonprofit accountability, and it's important that the information reported on the Form 990 accurately reflects the organization's financial health and compliance with legal requirements.

The Form 990 includes several key sections you should be familiar with:

- Revenue and Expenses: This section provides a detailed breakdown of the organization's income and expenses, including contributions, grants, program service revenue, and other sources of income. It also includes a listing of expenses by category (e.g., salaries, rent, program costs). Understanding this section is crucial for ensuring accurate financial reporting.

- Compensation of Officers, Directors, and Key Employees: This section discloses the salaries and benefits paid to the organization's top leadership, including the CEO, board members, and other key employees. As the CEO, be aware of this information and ensure that it aligns with the organization's compensation policies.

- Program Service Accomplishments: Here, the organization must describe its most significant programs and how they further its mission. It's important that this section accurately reflects the organization's activities, as it highlights how the nonprofit is fulfilling its mission.

- Governance, Management, and Disclosure: This section provides information on the organization's governance practices, including the board composition, conflict-of-interest policies, and executive compensation processes. Understanding this section is important for ensuring compliance with nonprofit governance best practices.

- Schedule A: Public Charity Status and Public Support: This schedule determines whether the organization qualifies as a public charity or a private foundation. It includes information on the organization's public support, such as donations and grants, and calculates the percentage of public support received.

As the CEO, you should review the Form 990 before it is filed to ensure the information is accurate and complete. Work closely with your finance director or accountant to address any discrepancies or issues. Additionally, be prepared to discuss the Form 990 with your board and stakeholders, as it is a key document for demonstrating the organization's financial health and accountability.

The Importance of Financial Literacy for Nonprofit CEOs

Financial literacy is an essential skill for nonprofit CEOs. While you don't need to be an accountant or financial expert, having a solid understanding of basic financial principles is crucial. Being able to interpret financial statements, budgets, and tax forms will enable you to make informed decisions, communicate effectively with your board and stakeholders, and lead your organization toward financial sustainability.

Here are a few key areas of financial literacy that every nonprofit CEO should be familiar with:

- Understanding Financial Statements: Financial statements, including the balance sheet, income statement, and cash flow statement, provide a snapshot of the organization's financial health. You should be able to read and interpret these statements, understand the implications of the numbers, and identify areas of concern.

- Budgeting and Forecasting: Creating and managing a budget is one of the most important aspects of your role. You should be able to develop a realistic budget that aligns with the organization's goals and resources, monitor performance against the budget, and adjust as needed.

- Cash Flow Management: Cash flow is the lifeblood of any organization. Understanding cash flow management involves monitoring cash inflows and outflows, forecasting future cash needs, and managing reserves to meet obligations.

- Fundraising and Revenue Generation: As CEO, you play a key role in fundraising and revenue generation. This includes understanding your organization's funding sources, developing strategies to diversify income streams, and ensuring that fundraising efforts align with financial goals.

- Risk Management: Financial risk management involves identifying risks to your organization's financial health—such as changes in funding, economic downturns, or unexpected expenses—and developing strategies to mitigate those risks.

- Compliance and Reporting: Nonprofits are subject to a variety of legal and regulatory requirements, including filing the Form 990, maintaining proper financial records, and complying with donor restrictions. Understanding these requirements and ensuring compliance is essential to maintaining your organization's tax-exempt status.

If you're not already confident in your financial literacy, consider taking a course or seeking resources to build your skills. Many organizations offer training programs for nonprofit leaders that cover essential financial topics. Don't hesitate to seek advice from your finance director, accountant, or board treasurer—these individuals can be invaluable resources.

Mastering Your Numbers as a Nonprofit CEO

As a nonprofit CEO, understanding your numbers and managing your organization's finances are critical components of your role. By knowing your budget, engaging with your board on financial matters, planning for the unexpected, collaborating with staff, and understanding the IRS Form 990, you can ensure that your organization remains financially stable and accountable.

Financial literacy is not just a nice-to-have skill—it's essential to your success. By mastering your numbers, you can make informed decisions, lead your organization with confidence, and achieve your mission while maintaining the trust and support of your donors, board, and community.

Remember, your organization's financial health is a reflection of your leadership. By taking the time to understand and manage finances effectively, you'll be well-equipped to guide your organization toward long-term success and sustainability.

Chapter 9: What is Overhead and Why you need to Know it?

Imagine walking into an Apple store and saying, "Okay, I'll buy the new iPhone, but I'm only willing to pay half of the asking price. I want to see Apple's plan for sustainability over the next two years after this purchase. I would also like a list of all the other customers who have purchased this type of phone and what they paid. Then, I want a breakdown of how my purchase has impacted the local area. Oh, and I don't want any of my purchase to go toward salaries or overhead."

Sounds crazy, right? In a real Apple store, this person would likely be laughed at and asked to leave, possibly with a call to security. Yet, when it comes to nonprofits, many donors expect this kind of detailed accountability and transparency, often with even more restrictive conditions on how their donations are used.

Overhead has become a buzzword in the nonprofit world, often misunderstood and misinterpreted by the public. Many people see overhead as a necessary evil at best and a sign of inefficiency or wastefulness at worst.

But what is overhead really, and why is it important to understand?

Understanding Overhead

In the simplest terms, overhead refers to the ongoing administrative and operational costs required to run an organization. This includes things like rent, utilities, office supplies, salaries, and other costs not directly tied to the delivery of services or programs. For nonprofits, overhead also encompasses the costs of fundraising, marketing, and donor relations—essential activities that ensure the organization can continue its mission.

However, the perception of overhead in the nonprofit sector is often skewed. Many donors expect nonprofits to operate with minimal overhead, believing that the bulk of their donation should go directly to the cause. This expectation is rooted in a misunderstanding of how nonprofits operate and the true cost of delivering services.

Unlike for-profit businesses, which are expected to invest in infrastructure, marketing, and salaries to grow and succeed, nonprofits are often criticized for spending money on anything other than direct program costs. This double standard can be detrimental, leading nonprofits to underinvest in critical areas like technology, staff development, and strategic planning— all of which are essential for long-term success.

The 990 Form: A Tool for Transparency

One of the primary tools for understanding a nonprofit's finances is the IRS Form 990. This form, required to be filed annually by most tax-exempt organizations, provides a detailed breakdown of the organization's financials, including revenue, expenses, and overhead.

The Form 990 is a valuable resource for donors, researchers, and anyone interested in the financial health and operations of a nonprofit. It includes information on the organization's governance, compliance with tax requirements, and key financial data. Importantly, it also provides insight into the organization's overhead, including salaries, administrative costs, and fundraising expenses.

Understanding how to read and interpret a Form 990 is crucial for anyone looking to assess a nonprofit's effectiveness. It's important to look beyond the simple overhead ratio—the percentage of expenses that go toward administrative and fundraising costs versus program costs—and consider the broader context. For example, a nonprofit with a higher overhead ratio might be investing in strategic initiatives, like upgrading technology or expanding its fundraising efforts, that will ultimately increase its impact.

Using the 990 as a Tool

The Form 990 can be a powerful tool for both nonprofits and donors when used correctly. For nonprofits, it offers an opportunity to tell their financial story in a transparent and compelling way. By clearly outlining their expenses and explaining how overhead supports their mission, nonprofits can help donors understand the importance of investing in the organization's infrastructure.

For donors, the Form 990 provides a wealth of information that can inform their giving decisions. Rather than focusing solely on overhead, donors can use the 990 to assess the overall financial health of the organization, including its revenue streams, fundraising efficiency, and programmatic impact. This holistic approach to evaluating a nonprofit can lead to more informed and effective philanthropy.

The Role of Guidestar and Charity Navigator

Guidestar and Charity Navigator are two of the most prominent organizations that provide information and ratings on nonprofits. These platforms are invaluable for donors who want to make informed decisions about where to allocate their charitable dollars.

Guidestar, now part of Candid, offers a comprehensive database of nonprofit information, including access to Form 990s, financial data, and qualitative information about an organization's mission, programs, and leadership. Nonprofits can earn different levels of transparency seals based on the amount of information they share, ranging from Bronze to Platinum. These seals help donors quickly gauge the transparency and accountability of an organization.

Charity Navigator rates nonprofits based on their financial health, accountability, and transparency. Historically, Charity Navigator placed a strong emphasis on overhead ratios, contributing to the public perception that low overhead was synonymous with effectiveness. However, in recent years, Charity Navigator has broadened its evaluation criteria to include measures of impact and results, recognizing that overhead alone is not a sufficient indicator of a nonprofit's performance.

The Overhead Myth

In 2013, Dan Pallotta's TED Talk, *"The Way We Think About Charity is Dead Wrong,"* sparked a shift in how people view nonprofit overhead. Pallotta argued that nonprofits should be encouraged to invest in their own growth and capacity, much like for-profit businesses. He criticized the obsession with low overhead, suggesting that it prevents nonprofits from achieving their full potential. His talk was a wake-up call for many in the sector, sparking a broader conversation about how we evaluate and support nonprofits.

Shortly after Pallotta's TED Talk, the CEOs of Charity Navigator, Guidestar, and the BBB Wise Giving Alliance published a joint letter to the donors of America. This letter, known as the "Overhead Myth" letter, aimed to dispel the notion that overhead is inherently bad and should be minimized at all costs. The letter encouraged donors to focus on the bigger picture, including the nonprofit's transparency, governance, leadership, and, most importantly, its results.

The "Overhead Myth" has done much to change the conversation around nonprofit overhead, but the misconception persists. Many donors still believe that the best nonprofits are those with the lowest overhead, and nonprofits often feel pressured to minimize their administrative costs, sometimes to the detriment of their effectiveness.

Why Understanding Overhead Matters

Understanding overhead is crucial for anyone involved in the nonprofit sector, whether as a donor, board member, or staff member. Overhead is not a sign of inefficiency; it is a necessary part of running a successful organization. When nonprofits are forced to operate with minimal overhead, they may struggle to invest in the infrastructure, staff, and resources needed to achieve their mission.

For donors, understanding overhead means recognizing that a nonprofit's administrative and fundraising costs are essential investments in its long-term success. Rather than penalizing nonprofits for having overhead, donors should consider how that overhead supports the organization's ability to deliver on its mission. A nonprofit with a higher overhead ratio may be investing in technology that improves efficiency, hiring skilled staff who can increase impact, or developing new fundraising strategies that will lead to greater financial sustainability.

For nonprofits, understanding and communicating the importance of overhead is key to building trust with donors and ensuring the organization's long-term success. Nonprofits should be transparent about their overhead costs and explain how those costs contribute to their mission. This transparency can help shift the conversation away from a narrow focus on overhead and toward a more comprehensive understanding of what it takes to run a successful nonprofit.

The Bigger Picture

Overhead is just one piece of the puzzle when it comes to evaluating a nonprofit's effectiveness. While it's important to keep administrative costs in check, it's equally important to recognize that overhead is necessary for a nonprofit to achieve its mission. By focusing on the bigger picture—transparency, governance, leadership, and results—donors can make more informed decisions and support nonprofits in a way that allows them to thrive.

In the end, the goal of philanthropy is not to minimize overhead, but to maximize impact. By understanding and embracing the role of overhead in nonprofit organizations, we can help ensure that these organizations have the resources they need to make a real difference in the world. Whether you're a donor, a nonprofit leader, or simply someone who cares about making a positive impact, it's important to look beyond the numbers and consider the true cost of doing good.

Chapter 10: The Importance of Fundraising

As a new nonprofit CEO, one of your most critical responsibilities will be fundraising. It's no exaggeration to say that the financial health of your organization—and by extension, its ability to fulfill its mission—depends on your ability to secure the necessary funds. Fundraising isn't just about asking for money; it's about building relationships, telling compelling stories, and ensuring that every dollar raised is used effectively and ethically. In this chapter, we'll explore the various aspects of fundraising that you, as a new nonprofit CEO, need to understand and master.

The Art of Asking for Money: Telling Your Story

Fundraising is fundamentally about storytelling. At its core, asking for money is about sharing the story of your organization—its mission, its impact, and its vision for the future—and inviting others to be a part of that story. Donors don't just give to organizations; they give to causes they believe in, to missions that resonate with them, and to stories that move them.

As the CEO, you are the chief storyteller of your organization. You need to be able to articulate the mission in a way that is compelling and relatable. This means not just stating facts and figures but also sharing the human side of your work. Who are the people your organization serves? What are their challenges, and how is your organization making a difference in their lives? These are the stories that will resonate with potential donors and inspire them to give.

Direct Asks: Knowing Your Donors and How to Talk to Them

One of the most effective ways to raise funds is through direct asks—personally requesting donations from individuals or organizations. However, successful direct asks require a deep understanding of your donors. Not all donors are the same, and a one-size-fits-all approach to fundraising is unlikely to be effective.

To make a successful direct ask, you need to know who your donors are. This involves understanding their motivations, interests, and capacity to give. Some donors may be passionate about a specific program or initiative, while others may be more interested in supporting the organization as a whole. Some may prefer to give small amounts regularly, while others may be capable of making large, one-time gifts.

Understanding your donors also means knowing how to communicate with them. Tailor your message to resonate with their interests and motivations. For example, if you know that a donor is particularly interested in education, focus on the impact of your organization's educational programs when making your ask. If a donor values transparency and accountability, be prepared to discuss how their donation will be used and the outcomes it will support.

Personalization is key to effective fundraising. Whenever possible, use the donor's name, reference their previous support, and make it clear that you value their partnership in your organization's work. Donors want to feel appreciated and recognized for their contributions, and personalizing your communication is one of the best ways to achieve this.

Understanding the Donor Cultivation Cycle

Fundraising is not a one-time event; it's an ongoing process that involves building and nurturing relationships with donors over time. This process is often referred to as the donor cultivation cycle, and understanding it is essential for any nonprofit CEO.

The donor cultivation cycle typically involves the following stages:

- Identification: The first step is identifying potential donors. This could involve researching individuals, corporations, or foundations that have an interest in your organization's mission. You might also identify potential donors through networking, referrals, or outreach efforts.

- Cultivation: Once potential donors have been identified, the next step is cultivation—building a relationship with them. This involves engaging them with your organization's work, sharing stories of impact, and keeping them informed about your activities. Cultivation can take time, but it's a critical part of the process, as it helps to build trust and rapport with potential donors.

- Solicitation: After cultivating a relationship with a potential donor, the next step is solicitation—asking for a donation. This is where the direct ask comes into play. Depending on the relationship and the donor's capacity, the ask might be for a one-time gift, a recurring donation, or a major contribution.

- Recognition: After receiving a donation, it's important to recognize and thank the donor for their support. This could involve sending a personalized thank-you note, publicly acknowledging their contribution, or inviting them to a special event. Recognition is key to building donor loyalty and encouraging future giving.

- Stewardship: The final stage of the donor cultivation cycle is stewardship—maintaining and deepening the relationship with the donor over time. This involves keeping them informed about how their donation is being used, sharing updates on the organization's progress, and continuing to engage them in your work. Effective stewardship is essential for retaining donors and encouraging them to continue supporting your organization.

By understanding and following the donor cultivation cycle, you can build lasting relationships with your donors and create a sustainable funding base for your organization.

Events, Dinners, and Galas: Planning with Purpose

Fundraising events, such as dinners, galas, and auctions, are a popular way for nonprofits to raise money and engage supporters. However, not all events are created equal, and it's important to approach event planning with a clear understanding of the costs, benefits, and potential impact on your organization.

Before committing to any fundraising event, start by asking yourself a few key questions:

- What is the goal of the event? Are you trying to raise a specific amount of money? Build relationships with key donors? Raise awareness about your organization's work? Having a clear goal will help guide your planning and decision-making.

- What are the costs? Fundraising events can be expensive to host, and it's essential to have a clear understanding of the costs involved. This includes not only the direct costs of the event, such as venue rental, catering, and entertainment, but also the indirect costs, such as staff time and resources.

- What is the potential return on investment? Before moving forward with an event, estimate the potential revenue it could generate and compare it to the costs. If the event is likely to cost more to host than it will raise in funds, it may not be worth pursuing.

- Does the event align with your organization's mission? It's important to ensure that any fundraising event aligns with your organization's mission and values. For example, if your organization focuses on environmental sustainability, hosting a lavish, wasteful event might send the wrong message to your supporters.

- What is the opportunity cost? Consider what other fundraising opportunities or activities you might have to forgo in order to host the event. If the event will take significant time and resources away from other important work, it may not be the best use of your organization's efforts.

If, after careful consideration, you determine that a fundraising event is a good fit for your organization, it's important to plan it carefully to maximize its success. This involves setting a clear budget, securing sponsorships and donations to offset costs, and promoting the event to your supporters. It's also important to evaluate the event afterward to assess its success and identify any areas for improvement.

Setting Goals and Planning Ahead

Effective fundraising requires careful planning and goal-setting. As a new nonprofit CEO, it's important to take the time to develop a comprehensive fundraising plan that outlines your goals, strategies, and timelines for the year ahead.

Start by setting clear, measurable fundraising goals. These goals should be based on your organization's financial needs, as well as its capacity to raise funds. For example, if your organization needs to raise $500,000 to cover its operating expenses for the year, that should be your primary fundraising goal. You might also set secondary goals, such as increasing donor retention by 10% or securing 50 new monthly donors.

Once you've set your goals, develop a detailed plan for achieving them. This plan should include a mix of fundraising strategies, such as direct mail campaigns, online fundraising, grant writing, and events. For each strategy, outline the specific steps you'll take, the timeline for implementation, and the individuals or teams responsible for each task.

In addition to traditional fundraising strategies, don't forget to explore other potential revenue streams, such as planned gifts and bequests. Planned giving involves securing donations that are arranged in advance and typically given as part of a donor's estate. Bequests, in particular, can be a significant source of funding for nonprofits, but they require careful cultivation and stewardship to secure.

Learning How to Apply for Grants

Grants are a valuable source of funding for many nonprofits, but they require a specific skill set to secure. As a new CEO, it's important to understand the grant application process and what is expected of your organization if it receives a grant.

The first step in applying for grants is identifying potential funders. This might involve researching foundations, government agencies, and corporations that provide grants to organizations like yours. When identifying potential funders, consider their funding priorities, eligibility requirements, and the size of the grants they offer.

Once you've identified potential funders, the next step is preparing your grant application. This typically involves submitting a proposal that outlines your organization's mission, the project or program you're seeking funding for, and how the funds will be used. It's important to be clear and concise in your proposal, and to provide evidence of your organization's impact and capacity to deliver the proposed project.

If your organization is awarded a grant, it's essential to understand what is expected of you in terms of reporting and accountability. Most grant funders require recipients to submit regular reports on the progress of the funded project, as well as a final report at the end of the grant period. These reports typically include information on how the funds were spent, the outcomes achieved, and any challenges encountered along the way.

In addition to reporting requirements, it's important to maintain a positive relationship with your grant funders. This involves keeping them informed of your progress, acknowledging their support in your communications, and inviting them to visit your organization or attend events. Building strong relationships with grant funders can lead to continued funding and other opportunities in the future.

Avoiding Mission Creep: Staying True to Your North Star

One of the challenges that many nonprofit CEOs face is the temptation to pursue funding opportunities that fall outside the organization's mission or expertise. This phenomenon, known as mission creep, occurs when an organization takes on projects or activities that are not aligned with its core mission in order to secure funding.

While it can be tempting to chase after funding opportunities, especially in a competitive fundraising environment, it's important to avoid mission creep. Not all money is good for your organization, and taking on projects that don't align with your mission can dilute your impact, strain your resources, and confuse your supporters.

To avoid mission creep, it's essential to stay focused on your organization's mission and use it as your North Star when making decisions. Before pursuing any new funding opportunity, ask yourself whether it aligns with your mission and whether your organization has the capacity to deliver on the proposed project. If the answer is no, it's better to pass on the opportunity and focus on finding funding that supports your core work.

In addition to staying true to your mission, it's important to be transparent with your donors and supporters about how their contributions are being used. Donors give to organizations because they believe in the mission, and they want to see their money used to advance that mission. By staying focused on your mission and avoiding mission creep, you can build trust with your donors and ensure that your organization remains on a clear and focused path.

The CEO's Role in Fundraising

As a new nonprofit CEO, fundraising will be one of the most important aspects of your role. It's not just about securing the funds needed to keep the organization running—it's about building relationships, telling compelling stories, and ensuring that every dollar raised is used effectively and ethically.

By understanding your donors, following the donor cultivation cycle, planning and executing events with purpose, setting clear goals, and avoiding mission creep, you can build a sustainable fundraising strategy that supports your organization's mission and growth.

Remember, fundraising is not just the responsibility of the development team—it's the responsibility of the entire organization, and as the CEO, you play a key role in leading these efforts. By embracing fundraising as a core part of your role and leading by example, you can inspire your team, engage your donors, and ensure that your organization has the resources it needs to achieve its mission.

Chapter 11: Making an Impact: How to Drive and Demonstrate Success

As a new nonprofit CEO, your role is not just to manage the day-to-day operations of your organization but to make a tangible impact in the lives of those you serve. In the nonprofit sector, success is measured by the difference you make, and this requires being both impact-driven and data-informed. To achieve this, you must be able to clearly articulate and demonstrate what your organization is accomplishing, not only to your board and donors but to the community at large.

This chapter will explore the importance of being impact-driven, the necessity of knowing your numbers, and how to utilize the "Logic Model" to effectively plan, execute, and measure the outcomes of your programs. By understanding these concepts, you can ensure that your organization is not only fulfilling its mission but doing so in a way that is both effective and accountable.

The Imperative of Being Impact-Driven

Nonprofits exist to make a difference. Whether you're working to alleviate poverty, protect the environment, or provide educational opportunities, your organization's mission is centered on creating positive change. However, it's not enough to simply have good intentions. In today's world, donors, funders, and stakeholders are increasingly demanding evidence of the impact their contributions are making. This means that as a nonprofit CEO, you must ensure that your organization is impact-driven.

Being impact-driven means that your organization's activities are focused on achieving specific, measurable outcomes that align with your mission. It involves setting clear goals, tracking progress, and being transparent about your successes and challenges. It also means being willing to adapt and improve your programs based on the data you collect.

For a nonprofit to be truly impact-driven, this mindset must permeate every aspect of the organization—from the programs you run to the way you communicate with donors and the metrics you use to measure success. As the CEO, it's your responsibility to foster this culture of impact within your organization and to ensure that everyone, from your board to your frontline staff, understands the importance of driving and demonstrating real, measurable results.

Knowing Your Numbers: The Foundation of Impact

To be impact-driven, you must first know your numbers. This means understanding the key metrics that define success for your organization and being able to track and report on them consistently. Knowing your numbers is crucial for making informed decisions, securing funding, and demonstrating your organization's impact to stakeholders.

Start by identifying the key performance indicators (KPIs) that are most relevant to your organization's mission. These might include metrics related to service delivery, program outcomes, financial performance, or community engagement. For example, if your organization provides job training for underserved populations, your KPIs might include the number of individuals trained, the percentage of participants who secure employment after completing the program, and the long-term job retention rates of those participants.

Once you've identified your KPIs, establish systems for collecting and analyzing data. This might involve implementing a data management system, training staff on data collection and reporting procedures, or partnering with external evaluators to assess your programs. It's important to ensure that the data you collect is accurate, timely, and relevant to your organization's goals.

In addition to tracking KPIs, it's important to regularly review your organization's financial performance. This includes monitoring your budget, cash flow, and fundraising results. Financial metrics are a key part of understanding your organization's overall health and sustainability, and they can provide important context for interpreting your impact data.

Knowing your numbers is not just about tracking data —it's about using that data to make informed decisions and drive continuous improvement. By regularly reviewing your metrics, you can identify areas where your organization is excelling and areas where there may be room for growth. This data-driven approach will help you stay focused on your mission and ensure that your organization is making the greatest possible impact.

Understanding the Logic Model: A Framework for Planning and Evaluation

One of the most effective tools for planning, implementing, and evaluating your organization's programs is the Logic Model. The Logic Model is a systematic and visual way to present and share your understanding of the relationships among the resources you have to operate your program, the activities you plan, and the changes or results you hope to achieve. It serves as both a planning tool and an evaluation framework, helping you to ensure that your programs are aligned with your mission and are producing the desired outcomes.

The Logic Model consists of several key components: inputs, activities, outputs, outcomes, impact, and indicators. Let's break down each of these components and explore how they can help you drive and demonstrate your organization's impact.

Inputs: The Resources You Have

Inputs refer to the resources that your organization uses to run its programs. These can include financial resources (such as grants and donations), human resources (such as staff and volunteers), physical resources (such as facilities and equipment), and informational resources (such as data and research).

As a nonprofit CEO, it's important to have a clear understanding of the inputs required for each of your programs. This includes not only the resources currently available but also any additional resources that may be needed to achieve your goals. For example, if you're planning to expand a program, you'll need to consider the additional staff, funding, and materials required to support that growth.

Understanding your inputs is the first step in ensuring that your programs are adequately resourced and that you are maximizing the use of those resources. It also helps you to make the case for additional funding or support when needed.

Activities: What You Do

Activities are the actions your organization takes to achieve its goals. These can include services provided, educational programs offered, advocacy efforts, and more. In the Logic Model, activities are the means through which your organization uses its inputs to create outputs and outcomes.

When planning your programs, it's important to clearly define the activities involved and how they will contribute to your organization's mission. This includes identifying the specific tasks that need to be completed, the timeline for implementation, and the individuals or teams responsible for each activity.

It's also important to consider how your activities are connected to your desired outcomes. For example, if your goal is to improve literacy rates among children in your community, your activities might include offering after-school tutoring programs, distributing books, and conducting literacy workshops for parents. By clearly linking your activities to your outcomes, you can ensure that your programs are strategically designed to achieve your goals.

Outputs: The Direct Results of Your Activities

Outputs are the direct results of your organization's activities. They are typically quantifiable and can include things like the number of people served, the number of workshops held, or the amount of materials distributed.

Outputs are an important part of the Logic Model because they provide a concrete measure of what your organization is doing. However, it's important to remember that outputs alone do not indicate impact. While they tell you how much work is being done, they don't necessarily tell you whether that work is making a difference.

For example, if your organization provides job training, an output might be the number of individuals who complete the training program. While this is an important metric, it doesn't tell you whether those individuals went on to secure employment or improve their economic situation. To truly demonstrate impact, you need to go beyond outputs and look at outcomes.

Outcomes: The Changes You Create

Outcomes are the changes or benefits that result from your organization's activities. These changes can occur at the individual, community, or systemic level, and they are often categorized as short-term, medium-term, and long-term outcomes.

- Short-term outcomes are the immediate changes that occur as a result of your activities. For example, if your organization provides health education workshops, a short-term outcome might be an increase in participants' knowledge about healthy eating.

- Medium-term outcomes are the changes that occur as participants begin to apply what they've learned. For example, as a result of increased knowledge about healthy eating, participants might start making healthier food choices.

- Long-term outcomes are the ultimate changes that your organization is working to achieve. These are often the hardest to measure, as they may take years to materialize. In the health education example, a long-term outcome might be a reduction in obesity rates in the community.

As a nonprofit CEO, it's important to clearly define the outcomes you hope to achieve and to regularly assess whether your activities are leading to those outcomes. This requires collecting and analyzing data on the changes that are occurring as a result of your programs. It also involves being willing to adapt and refine your programs based on what you learn.

Impact: The Broader Difference You Make

Impact refers to the broader, long-term effects of your organization's work. It's the ultimate difference that you're trying to make in the world. While outcomes are focused on specific changes among the individuals or communities you serve, impact looks at the overall contribution your organization is making toward its mission.

Measuring impact can be challenging, as it often requires looking at data over an extended period and considering the influence of external factors. However, it's essential for demonstrating the value of your organization's work and for securing support from donors, funders, and other stakeholders.

For example, if your organization's mission is to reduce homelessness, your impact might be measured by a decrease in the number of homeless individuals in your community over several years. This impact would be the result of multiple outcomes, such as increased access to housing, improved job placement services, and enhanced support networks.

As a nonprofit CEO, it's important to keep your organization's impact front and center. While it's easy to get caught up in the day-to-day work of running programs and meeting immediate needs, always remember the bigger picture and the long-term difference you're trying to make.

Indicators: Measuring Success

Indicators are the specific measures or metrics that you use to track your organization's progress toward its outcomes and impact. They are the data points that provide evidence of the changes that are occurring as a result of your programs.

When selecting indicators, it's important to choose metrics that are both meaningful and measurable. This means identifying indicators that accurately reflect the changes you're trying to achieve and that can be reliably tracked over time.

For example, if your organization is focused on improving educational outcomes for low-income students, your indicators might include metrics such as test scores, graduation rates, and college enrollment rates. These indicators provide concrete evidence of the impact your programs are having on students' educational success.

It's also important to regularly review and update your indicators to ensure that they continue to align with your organization's goals and activities. As your programs evolve and new challenges arise, you may need to adjust your indicators to better capture the outcomes and impact you're working to achieve.

Putting the Logic Model into Practice

Now that you understand the components of the Logic Model, it's time to put it into practice. Using the Logic Model as a framework for planning and evaluation can help you ensure that your organization's programs are strategically designed and that you have a clear roadmap for achieving your goals.

Here's how to get started:

1. Define Your Mission and Goals: Begin by clearly articulating your organization's mission and the specific goals you want to achieve. These goals should be aligned with your mission and should serve as the foundation for your Logic Model.

2. Identify Your Inputs: Next, identify the resources you have available to support your programs. This includes financial resources, staff and volunteers, facilities, equipment, and any other inputs that are necessary for your work.

3. Plan Your Activities: Based on your inputs, plan the specific activities that your organization will undertake to achieve its goals. Be sure to clearly define each activity, including who will be responsible for it, the timeline for implementation, and how it will contribute to your desired outcomes.

4. Determine Your Outputs: For each activity, identify the direct results that you expect to achieve. These outputs should be quantifiable and should provide a clear measure of the work that is being done.

5. Define Your Outcomes: Next, define the short-term, medium-term, and long-term outcomes that you hope to achieve as a result of your activities. These outcomes should be specific, measurable, and aligned with your organization's mission.

6. Articulate Your Impact: Consider the broader impact that your organization is working to achieve. How will your outcomes contribute to lasting change in the community or society? This impact should be the ultimate goal that drives your work.

7. Select Your Indicators: Finally, select the specific indicators that you will use to measure your progress toward your outcomes and impact. These indicators should be meaningful, measurable, and regularly reviewed to ensure that they accurately reflect your organization's success.

By following these steps, you can create a Logic Model that provides a clear and comprehensive framework for your organization's work. This model will not only guide your planning and implementation but will also serve as a valuable tool for evaluating your impact and communicating your success to stakeholders.

Communicating Your Impact

Once you've put the Logic Model into practice and started tracking your organization's progress, it's important to communicate your impact to your stakeholders. This includes your board, donors, funders, volunteers, and the broader community.

Effective communication is key to building trust and securing support for your organization. When communicating your impact, be sure to:

- Tell Your Story: Use the data you've collected to tell a compelling story about the difference your organization is making. Highlight both the quantitative and qualitative aspects of your impact, and share stories of individuals or communities that have benefited from your work.

- Be Transparent: Be honest and transparent about your successes and challenges. Donors and stakeholders appreciate organizations that are open about their progress and willing to learn from their experiences.

- Showcase Your Results: Use your indicators and metrics to showcase the results of your work. This might involve creating impact reports, infographics, or presentations that clearly illustrate your outcomes and impact.

- Engage Your Stakeholders: Invite your stakeholders to be a part of your impact journey. Share regular updates on your progress, solicit feedback, and involve them in your decision-making processes.

-

By effectively communicating your impact, you can build a strong case for support and inspire others to join you in achieving your mission.

Leading with Impact

As a new nonprofit CEO, your role is not just to lead your organization but to ensure that it is making a meaningful and measurable impact. By being impact-driven, knowing your numbers, and using the Logic Model to plan and evaluate your work, you can ensure that your organization is fulfilling its mission and creating lasting change.

Remember, making an impact is not just about doing good—it's about doing good well. By approaching your work with a focus on outcomes, evidence, and accountability, you can lead your organization to success and make a real difference in the lives of those you serve.

Chapter 12: Lead Your Staff: The Art of Leadership

As a new nonprofit CEO, one of your most significant responsibilities is leading your staff. While managing the day-to-day operations of your organization is crucial, true leadership goes beyond management. It involves inspiring, motivating, and setting the tone for the entire organization. Your ability to lead effectively will determine not only the success of your organization but also the morale, productivity, and satisfaction of your team.

This chapter explores the nuances of leadership versus management, the importance of communication, how to build the right organizational culture, the necessity of addressing issues promptly, the value of being a coach, and the importance of succession planning. By mastering these aspects of leadership, you can create a thriving work environment that empowers your staff and drives your organization's mission forward.

Leading vs. Managing: Understanding the Difference

As a new CEO, it's essential to recognize the difference between leading and managing. While these terms are often used interchangeably, they represent distinct approaches to working with your staff.

Management is primarily about processes, systems, and tasks. It involves organizing resources, setting goals, monitoring progress, and ensuring that day-to-day operations run smoothly. Managers focus on efficiency, consistency, and achieving specific outcomes. They are responsible for making sure that everything is done correctly and on time.

Leadership, on the other hand, is about people and vision. Leaders inspire and motivate their team, set the direction for the organization, and create a sense of purpose. They focus on the big picture and long-term goals, guiding their team toward achieving the organization's mission. While managers ensure that tasks are completed, leaders ensure that the right tasks are being pursued and that the team is engaged and committed to the organization's vision.

As a CEO, you need to be both a leader and a manager, but it's crucial to understand when to lead and when to manage. While you must ensure that the organization's operations are efficient and effective, your primary role is to lead your staff, inspire them, and create an environment where they can thrive.

Be a Leader: Inspire and Set the Tone

As the CEO, you are not just the head of the organization on the org chart—you are the leader who sets the tone for the entire organization. Your actions, decisions, and communication style will shape the culture and influence how your staff approaches their work.

To be an effective leader, you need to inspire your team. This involves sharing a compelling vision for the future, demonstrating passion for the organization's mission, and showing genuine care for your staff's well-being and professional development. When your team sees that you are committed to the organization's success and to their growth, they are more likely to be motivated and engaged in their work.

Setting the tone also means modeling the behavior you want to see in your staff. If you expect your team to be collaborative, open-minded, and innovative, you need to demonstrate these qualities yourself. Lead by example, and your team will follow your lead.

In addition to setting the tone, it's important to create an environment where your staff feels empowered to take initiative, share ideas, and contribute to the organization's success. This means fostering a culture of trust, respect, and accountability. When your team feels supported and valued, they are more likely to go above and beyond in their work.

Communicate, Communicate, and Communicate

Communication is the lifeblood of effective leadership. As the CEO, your ability to communicate clearly, consistently, and transparently will have a significant impact on your organization's success.

Effective communication starts with being clear about your expectations, goals, and vision. Your staff needs to understand what you want to achieve and how they can contribute to those goals. This means being explicit about the organization's priorities, the role of each team member, and the outcomes you expect.

In addition to setting expectations, it's important to keep your team informed about what's happening in the organization. This includes sharing updates on key initiatives, celebrating successes, and being honest about challenges or setbacks. When your team is well-informed, they are better equipped to do their jobs and feel more connected to the organization's mission.

Communication is not just about talking—it's also about listening. As a leader, you need to be open to feedback from your staff and willing to listen to their concerns, ideas, and suggestions. Create opportunities for open dialogue, whether through regular team meetings, one-on-one check-ins, or anonymous surveys. When your team feels heard, they are more likely to be engaged and motivated.

Finally, remember that communication is an ongoing process. It's not enough to have a single conversation or send out a one-time memo. You need to communicate regularly and consistently to ensure that everyone is on the same page and that your team remains aligned with the organization's goals.

Building the Right Culture: Culture Eats Strategy for Breakfast

There's an old saying in the business world: "Culture eats strategy for breakfast." This means that no matter how well-crafted your strategic plan is, it will fail if your organization's culture doesn't support it. As the CEO, building the right culture is one of your most important responsibilities.

Organizational culture is the set of shared values, beliefs, and norms that influence how people work together and how they approach their tasks. A positive culture can lead to increased employee engagement, higher productivity, and better outcomes for your organization. Conversely, a negative culture can result in low morale, high turnover, and poor performance.

To build the right culture, start by defining the core values that you want your organization to embody. These values should align with your mission and vision and should be reflected in everything you do. For example, if your organization values collaboration, make sure that your systems, processes, and leadership style encourage teamwork and open communication.

Once you've defined your values, it's important to integrate them into your daily operations. This means hiring staff who align with your values, recognizing and rewarding behaviors that support your culture, and addressing behaviors that undermine it. It also means being intentional about how you communicate, make decisions, and resolve conflicts.

Remember that culture is not static—it evolves over time based on the actions and behaviors of everyone in the organization. As the CEO, you play a key role in shaping and maintaining your organization's culture. By leading with your values and creating an environment where your staff feels supported and valued, you can build a culture that drives your organization's success.

Stop the Drama ASAP

In any organization, drama can be a significant distraction and can undermine your efforts to build a positive culture. Drama can take many forms, from interpersonal conflicts and gossip to power struggles and negativity. As the CEO, it's important to address drama promptly and effectively to prevent it from spreading and damaging your organization.

The first step in stopping drama is to create a culture of open communication and transparency. When your team feels comfortable speaking up and sharing their concerns, they are less likely to engage in behind-the-scenes drama. Encourage your staff to address issues directly with the people involved and to seek resolution through constructive dialogue.

If drama does arise, address it head-on. Don't ignore it or hope it will go away on its own. Meet with the individuals involved, listen to their perspectives, and work together to find a solution. Be clear about your expectations for behavior and the consequences of continued drama.

In some cases, drama may be a symptom of underlying issues, such as unclear roles, unmet needs, or a lack of accountability. If this is the case, take steps to address the root causes of the drama. This might involve clarifying responsibilities, providing additional support or resources, or reinforcing the organization's values and expectations.

Finally, lead by example. Model the behavior you want to see in your team, and avoid engaging in or tolerating drama yourself. By fostering a culture of respect, transparency, and accountability, you can minimize drama and create a more positive and productive work environment.

Be a Coach: Train, Equip, and Get Out of Their Way

As a CEO, one of your most important roles is to be a coach to your staff. This means providing them with the training, resources, and support they need to succeed, and then empowering them to take ownership of their work.

Being a coach starts with investing in your staff's development. This involves providing opportunities for training, professional development, and skill-building. Whether it's through formal training programs, mentorship, or on-the-job learning, make sure your team has the tools and knowledge they need to excel in their roles.

Equipping your staff also means ensuring they have the resources and support they need to do their jobs effectively. This might involve providing the right technology, allocating sufficient budget, or giving them access to the expertise they need. Make sure your team has what they need to succeed, and remove any obstacles that might stand in their way.

Once your team is trained and equipped, it's important to give them the autonomy to do their work. Micromanaging can stifle creativity, reduce motivation, and hinder productivity. Instead, trust your team to make decisions, take risks, and innovate. Provide guidance and support when needed, but give them the space to take ownership of their work.

As a coach, your role is to guide, support, and empower your team—not to do their work for them. By investing in your staff's development, equipping them with the resources they need, and giving them the autonomy to lead, you can create a high-performing team that drives your organization's success.

Succession Planning: Preparing for the Future

Succession planning is a critical aspect of leadership that is often overlooked. As the CEO, it's important to plan for the future by identifying and developing the next generation of leaders within your organization. This ensures that your organization remains strong and stable, even if key leaders, including yourself, leave or retire.

Succession planning involves several key steps:

1. Identify Potential Leaders: Start by identifying individuals within your organization who have the potential to take on leadership roles in the future. Look for staff members who demonstrate

strong leadership skills, a commitment to the organization's mission, and the ability to inspire and motivate others.

2. Develop Their Skills: Once you've identified potential leaders, invest in their development. Provide opportunities for training, mentorship, and leadership development. Encourage them to take on new challenges, lead projects, and gain experience in different areas of the organization.

3. Create a Leadership Pipeline: Develop a leadership pipeline by identifying the skills and experiences needed for key leadership roles and creating a plan to help potential leaders gain those skills and experiences. This might involve creating a leadership development program, offering cross-training opportunities, or providing access to external leadership development resources.

4. Plan for Your Own Succession: Succession planning isn't just about preparing others for leadership roles—it's also about planning for your own eventual departure. This means being honest with yourself and your board about your career goals and timeline, and ensuring that the organization is prepared for a smooth transition when the time comes.

5. Communicate Your Plan: Be transparent about your succession plan with your board and key stakeholders. This helps ensure that everyone is on the same page and that there is a clear plan in place for leadership transitions.

Succession planning is an ongoing process, not a one-time event. It's important to regularly review and update your succession plan to ensure that it remains relevant and that your organization is prepared for the future. By investing in leadership development and planning for the future, you can ensure that your organization remains strong and successful for years to come.

Leading with Purpose and Vision

As a new nonprofit CEO, leading your staff is one of the most important and challenging aspects of your role. By understanding the difference between leading and managing, inspiring your team, communicating effectively, building the right culture, addressing issues promptly, coaching your staff, and planning for the future, you can create a positive and productive work environment that empowers your team and drives your organization's mission forward.

Remember, leadership is not just about having a title or being in charge—it's about inspiring and guiding others to achieve a shared vision. By leading with purpose and vision, you can create a thriving organization that makes a lasting impact on the community you serve.

Chapter 13: Getting Your Message Out

As a new nonprofit CEO, one of your most critical tasks is getting your message out to the community, your stakeholders, and the broader public. The effectiveness with which you communicate your vision, your organization's mission, and your personal commitment can significantly impact your success and the success of your nonprofit. In this chapter, we will explore strategies for leveraging the initial "honeymoon period" of your tenure, utilizing various media outlets, engaging in public speaking and community events, and navigating the pros and cons of using social media as a nonprofit leader.

The Honeymoon Period: Use It While You Have It

The initial phase of your leadership—often referred to as the "honeymoon period"—is a time when you are likely to receive more attention, goodwill, and support than usual. Stakeholders, staff, and the community are typically eager to hear from you, and there is a natural curiosity about your vision and plans for the organization. However, this period is often short-lived, and it's essential to make the most of it while you have it.

During the honeymoon period, you have a unique opportunity to set the tone for your leadership and establish yourself as the face of the organization. This is the time to introduce yourself to key stakeholders, communicate your vision, and begin building relationships that will be crucial to your success. It's also a time to listen—gather feedback from staff, board members, donors, and the community to better understand their expectations and concerns.

To maximize the impact of the honeymoon period, consider the following strategies:

- Communicate Early and Often: Take advantage of the heightened interest in your leadership by communicating frequently with your stakeholders. This could include a series of introductory meetings, a welcome letter to donors, or a public announcement of your goals and vision for the organization.
- Establish Your Presence: Make a concerted effort to be visible both within your organization and in the community. Attend events, visit programs, and meet with staff and volunteers. Your presence will help build trust and signal that you are actively engaged in the organization's work.
- Set Clear Expectations: Use the honeymoon period to establish clear expectations for your leadership. This might include outlining your priorities for the first 100 days, setting goals for the organization, or communicating your values and leadership style. By setting expectations early, you can help guide the organization's direction and focus.

- Leverage Media Attention: The media is often interested in covering leadership transitions, especially for high-profile nonprofits. Use this attention to your advantage by reaching out to local media outlets, offering interviews, and sharing your vision for the organization. This can help raise awareness of your leadership and generate positive publicity for your nonprofit.

You, Your Message, and Beyond the Organization's Methods

As the CEO, your message is a powerful tool for shaping the perception of your organization. However, it's important to recognize that your message extends beyond the formal communications of the organization —it's also about how you present yourself, how you interact with others, and how you integrate your role into your everyday life.

Your message is a reflection of who you are as a leader and what you stand for. It's not just about what you say, but how you say it and the actions you take. To effectively communicate your message, consider the following:

- Be Authentic: Authenticity is key to building trust and credibility. Be true to yourself and your values, and let that authenticity come through in your communications. Whether you're speaking at an event, writing an op-ed, or posting on social media, your message should reflect who you are and what you believe in.

- Align Your Message with the Mission: Your personal message should be closely aligned with the mission of your organization. When you speak about your organization's work, make sure that your message reinforces the organization's goals and values. This consistency will help strengthen the connection between you and your organization in the eyes of your stakeholders.
- Be Strategic: While it's important to be authentic, it's also important to be strategic in how you communicate. Consider your audience and the impact you want to have. Tailor your message to resonate with different groups—whether it's donors, volunteers, or the general public—and choose the right channels to reach them.
- Lead by Example: Your actions as a leader speak as loudly as your words. Demonstrate your commitment to the organization's mission through your actions, whether it's volunteering alongside staff, attending community events, or advocating for the cause. Your leadership will be more impactful when it's backed by visible, consistent action.

Leveraging Local Media: Your Voice in the Community

Local media outlets—such as newspapers, radio stations, and television shows—are valuable platforms for getting your message out to the community. As a nonprofit leader, you can use these channels to raise awareness of your organization's work, share your vision, and build relationships with the broader public.

Here are some ways to effectively use local media to share your message:

- Press Releases: Press releases are a traditional but effective way to communicate important news about your organization, such as new initiatives, upcoming events, or leadership changes. Make sure your press releases are well-written, timely, and newsworthy to increase the chances of them being picked up by local media.
- Local Radio and Television: Many local radio stations and television programs, especially those with a focus on community affairs, are open to featuring nonprofit leaders on their shows. Reach out to local radio stations or Sunday morning talk shows and offer to discuss your organization's work, upcoming events, or issues related to your cause. These appearances can help you reach a wider audience and establish yourself as a leader in the community.
- Op-Eds and Letters to the Editor: Writing op-eds or letters to the editor can be a powerful way to share your perspective on issues relevant to your organization's mission. These pieces allow you to advocate for your cause, raise awareness of your organization's work, and share your vision with a broad audience. When writing an op-ed, be sure to focus on a specific issue, offer a clear argument, and back up your points with evidence.
- Build Relationships with Journalists: Building relationships with local journalists can help you get your message out more effectively. Reach out to reporters who cover issues related to your

organization and offer to be a source of information or commentary. By establishing yourself as a reliable and knowledgeable contact, you can increase the likelihood of your organization being featured in local news stories.

Public Speaking and Community Engagement: Know Your Target Audience

Public speaking and community engagement are powerful tools for raising awareness of your organization's work and building relationships with key stakeholders. Whether you're speaking at a Rotary Club meeting, attending a community event, or participating in a panel discussion, these opportunities allow you to share your message directly with your target audience.

Here's how to make the most of public speaking and community engagement:

- Know Your Audience: Before speaking at an event or engaging with a community group, take the time to understand your audience. What are their interests, concerns, and values? How does your organization's work align with their priorities? By tailoring your message to resonate with your audience, you can make a more meaningful connection and increase the impact of your message.
- Be Clear and Concise: When speaking in public, it's important to be clear, concise, and to the point. Avoid jargon or overly complex language, and focus on delivering a message that is easy to understand and remember. Practice your speech

in advance to ensure that you stay within the allotted time and effectively convey your key points.
- Tell Stories: Stories are one of the most powerful ways to connect with an audience. Share stories about the people your organization serves, the impact of your programs, or your own personal experiences related to the cause. Stories can help humanize your message, evoke emotion, and make your message more memorable.
- Engage with the Community: Beyond speaking engagements, look for opportunities to engage with the community in a more informal setting. Attend local events, volunteer alongside community members, and participate in discussions related to your cause. These interactions can help you build relationships, gain insights into the community's needs, and establish yourself as a trusted leader.
- Follow Up: After speaking at an event or engaging with a community group, be sure to follow up. Send a thank you note to the event organizers, reach out to individuals you met, and continue the conversation through email or social media. Following up shows that you value the opportunity to connect and helps keep your organization top of mind.

Becoming the "Go-To" Person for Your Organization

As the CEO, you are the face and voice of your organization. It's important to establish yourself as the "go-to" person for all things related to your nonprofit.

This means being available, accessible, and knowledgeable about your organization's work and the issues it addresses.

To become the go-to person for your organization, consider the following strategies:

- Be Visible: Make sure that you are visible both within and outside of your organization. Attend meetings, events, and community gatherings. Be present in the office and approachable to staff and volunteers. The more visible you are, the more people will see you as the leader and spokesperson for your organization.
- Be Informed: Stay informed about the latest developments in your organization and the broader sector. This includes being up to date on your organization's programs, finances, and strategic goals, as well as being knowledgeable about trends, challenges, and opportunities in the nonprofit sector. Your ability to speak confidently and knowledgeably about your organization will strengthen your credibility as a leader.
- Build Relationships with Key Stakeholders: Establish strong relationships with key stakeholders, including board members, donors, community leaders, and media contacts. These relationships will help you stay informed, build support for your organization, and position yourself as the go-to person for information and updates.
- Respond Promptly: When someone reaches out to you—whether it's a journalist, donor, or community member—respond promptly and

professionally. Being responsive shows that you are engaged and committed to your role as a leader. It also helps build trust and encourages others to turn to you for information and guidance.
- Communicate Regularly: Keep your stakeholders informed through regular communications, such as newsletters, email updates, and social media posts. Consistent communication helps reinforce your role as the go-to person and keeps your organization's work top of mind.

Social Media: Pros and Cons for a Nonprofit Leader

Social media is a powerful tool for sharing your message, building your personal brand, and engaging with your community. However, it also comes with potential pitfalls, especially for nonprofit leaders. Understanding the pros and cons of using social media as a nonprofit CEO can help you navigate this landscape effectively.

Pros of Using Social Media:

- Reach a Broader Audience: Social media platforms like Facebook, Twitter, LinkedIn, and Instagram allow you to reach a wide audience quickly and efficiently. You can share updates, promote events, and engage with supporters in real-time.

- Humanize Your Leadership: Social media gives you the opportunity to show a more personal side of your leadership. You can share behind-the-scenes insights, highlight your involvement in the community, and connect with followers on a more personal level.
- Engage with Supporters: Social media allows for two-way communication, enabling you to interact directly with your supporters. You can respond to comments, answer questions, and engage in conversations that build stronger relationships.
- Amplify Your Message: Social media can help amplify your message, especially when content is shared, liked, or commented on by your followers. This can increase your reach and raise awareness of your organization's work.

Cons of Using Social Media:

- Time-Consuming: Maintaining an active social media presence can be time-consuming. It requires regular posting, monitoring of comments and messages, and engagement with followers. For busy nonprofit CEOs, this can be a significant commitment.
- Risk of Miscommunication: Social media is a public platform, and there's always a risk that something you post could be misinterpreted or taken out of context. This can lead to negative publicity or misunderstandings.

- Blurring of Personal and Professional Lines: As a nonprofit leader, your personal social media presence is often intertwined with your professional role. This can blur the lines between your personal and professional life, and it's important to be mindful of what you share and how it reflects on your organization.
- Potential for Negative Feedback: Social media platforms are open forums, and not all feedback will be positive. You may encounter criticism, negative comments, or even attacks on your organization. It's important to be prepared to handle these situations professionally. Please know, that any response to these trolls, might make it worse.

Best Practices for Using Social Media as a Nonprofit CEO:

- Be Authentic: Just as with other forms of communication, authenticity is key on social media. Be genuine in your interactions and let your personality shine through.

- Maintain Professionalism: While it's important to be authentic, it's also important to maintain professionalism. Be mindful of the content you share and how it reflects on your organization.
- Engage with Followers: Social media is about engagement. Take the time to respond to comments, answer questions, and interact with your followers. This helps build a sense of community and shows that you value your supporters.

- Be Consistent: Consistency is important for building a strong social media presence. Develop a content strategy that includes regular posts and updates, and stick to it.
- Monitor and Manage: Keep an eye on what's being said about you and your organization on social media. Address any negative feedback promptly and professionally, and use social media monitoring tools to stay informed.

Crafting and Sharing Your Message as a Nonprofit CEO

As a new nonprofit CEO, getting your message out is one of the most important aspects of your role. By leveraging the honeymoon period, crafting a personal and authentic message, utilizing local media, engaging in public speaking and community events, establishing yourself as the go-to person for your organization, and navigating the pros and cons of social media, you can effectively communicate your vision, build strong relationships, and raise awareness of your organization's work.

Remember, communication is not just about what you say—it's about how you say it, where you say it, and how consistently you reinforce your message. By being strategic, authentic, and proactive in your communications, you can make a lasting impact as a leader and drive your organization's mission forward.

Chapter 14: The Power of Thank You and Recognition

As a new nonprofit CEO, one of the most powerful tools at your disposal is the simple act of saying "thank you." Gratitude and recognition are not just niceties—they are essential for building strong relationships, fostering a positive organizational culture, and encouraging ongoing support from donors, staff, board members, and volunteers. In a sector where success often hinges on the goodwill and commitment of others, mastering the art of gratitude can significantly impact your organization's sustainability, growth, and reputation.

This chapter explores the profound importance of saying thank you, the different ways to express gratitude, and how to tailor your recognition efforts to the preferences of those you are thanking. By understanding and leveraging the power of thank you, you can strengthen your relationships with key stakeholders and create an environment where everyone feels valued and motivated to contribute.

Understanding Preferences: Knowing How People Like to Be Thanked

One of the first lessons in effective recognition is understanding that people have different preferences when it comes to how they like to be thanked. For some, public recognition is highly valued—they may appreciate having their name listed in the annual report, receiving a plaque to hang in their office, or being acknowledged in front of their peers at a special event. For others, however, recognition is a more private matter—they may prefer a quiet thank you or no recognition at all, particularly if they value discretion or are motivated by the cause itself rather than public acknowledgment.

As the CEO, it's important to get to know the individuals you're working with—whether they're donors, staff, board members, or volunteers—and understand how they prefer to be recognized. This might involve asking them directly, observing their reactions to past recognition efforts, or simply building enough rapport to gauge their preferences intuitively.

For example, some donors might relish the opportunity to have a room or program named after them, while others might shy away from any public acknowledgment of their gift. Similarly, some staff members might thrive on public praise during team meetings, while others might feel uncomfortable and prefer a private thank you note or gesture.

Tailoring your recognition efforts to individual preferences shows that you value and respect the people who support your organization. It ensures that your gratitude is received in the way it is intended, making it more meaningful and impactful. Knowing your audience in this way is not just an act of good leadership—it's an act of respect and thoughtful relationship-building that will serve your organization well in the long run.

Publicly Thanking Your Staff, Board Members, and Volunteers

Public recognition is a powerful way to show appreciation and boost morale within your organization. When done thoughtfully, it can reinforce positive behavior, strengthen relationships, and create a culture of gratitude and mutual respect. Moreover, public acknowledgment serves as a signal to the broader team about what the organization values—whether it's dedication, creativity, or teamwork—and sets a positive example for others to follow.

One of the most effective ways to publicly thank your staff, board members, and volunteers is by acknowledging their contributions in meetings, newsletters, or at events. For example, you might start a board meeting by thanking a member for their leadership on a recent initiative, or you could highlight the efforts of a volunteer team in your organization's newsletter.

It's important to make public recognition a regular practice rather than a one-time event. By consistently acknowledging the hard work and dedication of your team, you create an environment where people feel valued and motivated to continue contributing. This is especially important in the nonprofit sector, where many staff and volunteers are driven by a passion for the cause rather than financial compensation.

In addition to formal recognition, consider more informal opportunities to publicly thank your team. For example, you might send out a quick email to the entire staff acknowledging the extra effort someone put into a project, or you might take a moment during a casual team gathering to express your appreciation for a job well done.

Public recognition should be specific and sincere. Rather than giving generic praise, take the time to acknowledge the specific actions or qualities that you are grateful for. For example, instead of simply saying, "Thank you for your hard work," you might say, "I really appreciate the way you took the initiative to lead the planning for our annual fundraiser. Your creativity and attention to detail made it a huge success." This level of specificity shows that you are truly paying attention and that your gratitude is genuine.

Private Recognition: The Power of a Personal Thank You

While public recognition is important, private recognition can be equally powerful, especially for those who prefer a more personal approach. Private thank yous can take many forms, from handwritten notes to small tokens of appreciation, and they are an effective way to show that you care about the individual and their contribution.

One of the most meaningful ways to thank someone privately is by writing a handwritten note. In today's digital world, handwritten notes are increasingly rare, which makes them stand out even more. Taking the time to write a personal message shows that you've put thought and effort into your gratitude, and it leaves a lasting impression.

When writing a thank you note, be sure to make it specific and personal. Mention the specific actions or qualities you are grateful for, and explain why they made a difference to you or the organization. For example, you might write, "Dear Sara, I wanted to take a moment to thank you for the incredible work you did on our recent donor event. Your attention to detail and ability to keep everything running smoothly was truly impressive, and I know our donors felt valued and appreciated because of your efforts."

Small gestures like allowing someone to leave early, offering a public shout-out, or sending a special gift can also be meaningful ways to express private gratitude. These moments, though often quieter, create bonds of trust and goodwill that can be equally impactful.

The Importance of Thank You Notes: Making Gratitude Tangible

Thank you notes are a timeless and effective way to express gratitude. As a nonprofit CEO, they should be a regular part of your routine. Whether it's thanking a donor for their support, acknowledging a board member's leadership, or expressing appreciation for a staff member's hard work, a well-written thank you note can leave a lasting positive impression.

There are several situations where thank you notes are particularly appropriate:

- After a Donation: Whenever your organization receives a donation, it's important to send a thank you note as soon as possible. This not only shows your appreciation but also reinforces the donor's decision to support your organization. The note should be specific to the donor and their gift, and it should highlight the impact their donation will have on your work.

- After a Meeting or Introduction: If someone takes the time to meet with you, introduce you to a potential partner, or offer advice, a thank you note is a thoughtful way to acknowledge their effort. Even if the meeting doesn't immediately result in a partnership or donation, sending a note shows that you value their time and are grateful for their support.

- After an Event or Project: If a staff member, volunteer, or board member goes above and beyond on a project or event, a thank you note is a great way to recognize their hard work. This can be especially meaningful if the project required extra effort or was particularly challenging.

Leveraging Technology: Digital Thank Yous in the Modern Age

While handwritten notes and face-to-face thank yous remain impactful, technology also offers opportunities for modern expressions of gratitude. In today's fast-paced, digital-first world, sending a timely thank you via email or social media can be a powerful way to acknowledge someone's efforts, especially when speed and efficiency are critical.

For example, following a virtual meeting, sending a quick thank you email to all participants not only shows appreciation but also serves as a way to recap and reinforce key takeaways. Similarly, thanking volunteers or donors through social media can amplify their contributions while also engaging a broader audience.

Video messages are another effective tool. Recording a short video to personally thank someone can be more heartfelt and memorable than a simple email. It adds a personal touch, allowing the recipient to see and hear your appreciation.

While digital thank yous offer convenience and immediacy, balance them with more traditional methods when appropriate. Personal, thoughtful gestures will always leave the most lasting impression.

Creating a Culture of Gratitude: Organizational Benefits

Beyond individual thank yous, cultivating a broader culture of gratitude within your organization can have profound impacts on morale, productivity, and overall job satisfaction. When employees and volunteers feel appreciated, they are more likely to remain engaged, committed, and loyal to the organization.

As a CEO, you set the tone for the organization. By modeling gratitude in your daily interactions and encouraging others to do the same, you can help create an environment where everyone feels valued. This might include implementing formal recognition programs or simply encouraging managers to regularly acknowledge the efforts of their teams.

The Ripple Effect: How Gratitude Impacts Your Organization's Reputation

Gratitude doesn't just benefit your internal culture; it can also enhance your organization's reputation in the broader community. When people feel appreciated, they are more likely to speak positively about your organization, helping to attract new donors, volunteers, and partners.

Chapter 15: Mastering Time Management

As a new nonprofit CEO, you will quickly discover that time is one of your most valuable resources. With a multitude of responsibilities, meetings, events, and projects all demanding your attention, effective time management is crucial for your success. The ability to manage your calendar, prioritize tasks, and ensure that you're spending your time on what matters most will not only help you lead your organization more effectively but also maintain a healthy work-life balance.

This chapter delves into key strategies for mastering time management, including managing your calendar, blocking out time for focused work, scheduling regular check-ins with your team, planning for events and major projects, handling crises, and balancing personal and professional commitments. By implementing these practices, you can take control of your time, reduce stress, and lead your organization with greater clarity and efficiency.

Manage Your Calendar, or Your Calendar Will Manage You

One of the first rules of effective time management is to take control of your calendar. As a nonprofit CEO, your calendar will quickly fill up with meetings, events, and appointments, leaving little time for the deep work and strategic thinking that your role requires. If you don't actively manage your calendar, it will end up managing you.

To take control of your calendar, start by setting boundaries and priorities. Determine what is most important for you to focus on each day, week, and month, and schedule time for these activities before anything else. This might include time for strategic planning, one-on-one meetings with key staff members, or working on major projects. Prioritize the non-negotiables and delegate what you can.

One effective strategy is to color-code your calendar based on the type of activity. For example, you might use one color for meetings, another for focused work time, and another for personal commitments. This visual approach can help you quickly see how your time is being allocated and ensure that you're spending it on the right things.

Additionally, it's essential to regularly review and adjust your calendar. As new tasks and priorities arise, be willing to reschedule or delegate activities that are less important. Flexibility and adaptability are key to managing your time effectively in a dynamic and fast-paced environment.

Lastly, build in buffer times to prevent back-to-back commitments from overwhelming your day. These short breaks allow you to reflect, refocus, or recharge before moving on to your next task.

Block Out Time to Work: Avoid the Meeting Trap

Meetings are a necessary part of any CEO's job, but they can quickly take over your entire day if you're not careful. To avoid falling into the meeting trap, it's essential to block out time on your calendar for focused work.

Blocking out time means setting aside specific hours or even entire days where you're not available for meetings, phone calls, or other interruptions. During this time, you can focus on the deep work that requires your full attention, whether it's writing a strategic plan, reviewing financial statements, or developing new initiatives. Guard this time fiercely — it is often the most productive part of your schedule.

To make the most of your blocked work time, be intentional about how you use it. Identify your most important tasks and prioritize them during these periods. Eliminate distractions by turning off notifications, closing your email, and finding a quiet place to work if possible. If you work remotely, designate an area that signals "do not disturb" to others in your household.

If you find it challenging to carve out time for focused work, consider implementing "No Meeting Days" or "Quiet Hours" where meetings are discouraged or limited to urgent matters. Communicate these boundaries to your team so they understand that this time is essential for your productivity and the organization's success.

Remember Travel Time: Plan for the Gaps

As a nonprofit CEO, you will likely need to attend meetings, events, and lunches off-site. It's easy to forget to account for travel time between these commitments, which can lead to a rushed and stressful day. To avoid this, make sure to include travel time in your calendar.

When scheduling off-site meetings, consider the location and the time it will take to get there and back. Add buffer time around these appointments to account for potential delays, parking, or the need to prepare before the meeting. This will help you arrive on time, reduce stress, and ensure that you're fully present for each engagement.

Additionally, use travel time productively. If you have to commute, use it as an opportunity to make important calls, listen to industry podcasts, or review meeting notes. Treat this time as part of your workday, allowing you to stay productive even when you're on the move.

If possible, try to group off-site meetings in the same area on the same day to minimize travel time. For example, if you have multiple meetings in the same part of town, schedule them back-to-back so you can make the most efficient use of your time.

Schedule Regular Meetings with Your Direct Reports

Regular communication with your direct reports is essential for effective leadership and time management. Scheduling weekly or bi-weekly meetings with your key staff members provides a set time to discuss current projects, quarterly or annual goals, and any challenges or opportunities that arise. These meetings are also an opportunity to build relationships and trust with your team.

When scheduling these meetings, make sure they are a consistent part of your calendar. Having a regular time set aside for one-on-one meetings ensures that important issues are addressed promptly and that your direct reports have a clear understanding of your expectations and priorities.

During these meetings, focus on both operational and relational aspects. Discuss current projects and progress toward goals, but also take the time to ask about your team members' well-being, professional development, and any support they may need. Building a strong rapport with your direct reports can lead to better communication, increased trust, and a more cohesive team.

In addition to one-on-one meetings, consider holding regular team meetings where your direct reports can come together to discuss broader organizational goals, share updates, and collaborate on cross-functional projects. These meetings can help ensure alignment and foster a sense of teamwork and shared purpose.

Planning Events and Major Projects: Work Backwards from the End Date

Events and major projects are significant undertakings that require careful planning and coordination. To ensure success, it's important to work backwards from the end date, creating a detailed timeline that includes all key milestones, check-in meetings, and deadlines.

Start by identifying the final date when the event or project needs to be completed. Then, work backwards to establish when each major task or milestone needs to be accomplished. For example, if you're planning a fundraising gala, you might need to have the venue booked six months in advance, invitations sent out three months in advance, and final RSVPs confirmed one month before the event.

Once you have a timeline in place, schedule regular check-in and update meetings to monitor progress and address any issues that arise. These meetings ensure that everyone involved is on the same page, that tasks are completed on time, and that any potential problems are identified and resolved early.

It's also important to schedule pre- and post-event meetings to evaluate the planning and execution process. Pre-event meetings allow the team to identify any last-minute tasks or adjustments, while post-event meetings provide an opportunity to assess what went well and what could be improved for future events. This continuous improvement process is key to delivering successful events and projects.

Crisis Management: Everything Can Feel Like a Crisis

In the fast-paced world of nonprofit leadership, it can sometimes feel like everything is a crisis. Whether it's a funding shortfall, a staff issue, or an urgent request from a board member, there will always be challenges that demand your attention. However, not everything is truly a crisis, and effective time management requires the ability to prioritize and manage these situations appropriately.

One of the keys to crisis management is to remain calm and focused. When a situation arises, take a moment to assess its urgency and impact. Is it something that needs to be addressed immediately, or can it be scheduled for later in the day or week? By taking a step back and evaluating the situation, you can avoid being pulled into every urgent matter and maintain control over your time.

It's also important to have a plan in place for handling real crises. This might involve delegating tasks to your team, setting up a crisis management protocol, or having a list of key contacts to reach out to for support. By being prepared, you can respond more effectively and minimize the disruption to your schedule.

Balancing Personal and Professional Commitments: Family Comes First

As a nonprofit CEO, your professional responsibilities can be all-consuming. However, it's important to remember that your personal life and well-being are just as important. Balancing personal and professional commitments is essential for maintaining a healthy work-life balance and avoiding burnout.

One of the best ways to ensure that you prioritize your personal life is to put personal and family events on your calendar. Just as you would schedule a meeting or an important deadline, schedule time for birthdays, soccer matches, dance recitals, and date nights. By blocking off this time on your work calendar, you send a clear message to yourself and others that these commitments are non-negotiable.

It's also important to communicate your boundaries to your team and stakeholders. Let them know that you have personal commitments that are important to you and that you expect your time to be respected. By setting these boundaries early on, you can help create a culture of work-life balance within your organization.

In addition to scheduling personal events, make time for self-care and relaxation. Whether it's exercising, reading, or spending time with loved ones, make sure you have time each day or week to recharge. Taking care of yourself is essential for maintaining your energy, focus, and effectiveness as a leader.

Taking Control of Your Time as a Nonprofit CEO

Time management is one of the most critical skills for a nonprofit CEO. With so many demands on your time, it's essential to take control of your calendar, prioritize your tasks, and ensure that you're spending your time on what matters most.

By managing your calendar, blocking out time for focused work, planning for travel, scheduling regular meetings with your team, planning events and projects backwards from the end date, handling crises effectively, and balancing personal and professional commitments, you can lead your organization with greater clarity, efficiency, and purpose.

Remember, time is a finite resource, and how you choose to spend it will have a significant impact on your success and the success of your organization. Mastering time management not only helps you work more effectively but also improves your quality of life as you strive to maintain a balance between work and personal commitments.

Chapter 16: Taking Care of Yourself

As a new nonprofit CEO, you have likely already realized that the demands of your role are immense. You are responsible for leading your organization, supporting your staff, managing finances, building relationships with donors, and ensuring that your nonprofit fulfills its mission. With so many responsibilities, it's easy to focus all your energy on your work, often at the expense of your own well-being. However, one of the most important lessons you'll learn as a leader is that taking care of yourself is just as important as taking care of your organization.

Self-care is not a luxury or an indulgence—it is a critical component of effective leadership. In a role where you are constantly balancing the needs of your staff, board, donors, and the communities you serve, maintaining your physical, mental, and emotional health is essential for your success. Neglecting self-care can lead to burnout, compromised decision-making, and ultimately, the diminished capacity to drive your nonprofit's mission forward.

This chapter explores the importance of self-care for nonprofit CEOs and offers practical strategies for maintaining your physical, mental, and emotional health. By prioritizing your well-being, you will not only enhance your ability to lead effectively but also set a positive example for your staff and create a more sustainable work-life balance.

The Responsibility of Self-Care: Leading by Example

As a nonprofit CEO, you are responsible for the well-being of your staff, ensuring they have the support, resources, and environment they need to thrive. But it's equally important to recognize that you are also responsible for taking care of yourself. If you neglect your own health and well-being, you risk burnout, decreased effectiveness, and even physical and mental health issues.

The responsibility of self-care is not just about protecting your own well-being; it is also about leading by example. Your team looks to you for guidance on how to navigate the challenges of nonprofit work. When you prioritize self-care, you send a powerful message to your staff: that taking time for oneself is not only acceptable but necessary for long-term success. This can help create a culture where work-life balance is valued, reducing stress and improving overall job satisfaction within your organization.

As the leader of your organization, your energy, focus, and well-being directly impact your ability to make sound decisions, support your team, and drive your nonprofit's mission forward. Leading by example means showing your staff that it's okay to set boundaries, take breaks, and prioritize mental and physical health. This not only benefits you but also promotes a healthier organizational culture.

Taking care of yourself is not a luxury; it's a necessity. By investing in your own health and happiness, you are better equipped to lead your organization to success.

Physical Health: Making Time for Exercise and Movement

Physical health is the foundation of overall well-being. Regular exercise and movement are essential for maintaining energy levels, reducing stress, and improving mental clarity. However, with a demanding schedule, it can be challenging to find time for physical activity. That's why it's crucial to make exercise a priority and integrate it into your daily routine.

Here are some strategies for staying physically active as a busy nonprofit CEO:

1. Schedule Exercise Like a Meeting: Treat your workouts like any other important appointment on your calendar. Block out specific times for exercise, whether it's a morning walk, a lunchtime gym session, or an evening yoga class. By scheduling exercise, you make it a non-negotiable part of your day, just like meetings or deadlines.

2. Find Activities You Enjoy: Exercise doesn't have to be a chore. Find physical activities that you genuinely enjoy, whether it's swimming, cycling, dancing, or hiking. When you enjoy the activity, you're more likely to stick with it and look forward to it as a way to unwind. The key is to view exercise as an opportunity to de-stress, rather than another obligation.

3. Incorporate Movement into Your Day: If you have a particularly busy day, look for ways to incorporate movement into your routine. Take the stairs instead of the elevator, go for a walk during phone calls, or do some stretching exercises at your desk. Even small amounts of movement can add up and help you stay active.

4. Use Exercise as a Stress Reliever: Physical activity is a powerful stress reliever. When you're feeling overwhelmed or anxious, take a break to go for a walk or do a quick workout. This can help clear your mind, improve your mood, and boost your productivity when you return to work. Sometimes, the simple act of moving your body can shift your mindset and give you a fresh perspective.

5. Make It Social: Exercise can also be a way to connect with others. Consider joining a fitness class, running group, or sports team. Exercising with others can provide motivation, accountability, and a sense of community. Social exercise can be especially beneficial for nonprofit CEOs, who may feel isolated in their leadership roles.

By prioritizing physical health, you'll have more energy, better focus, and a stronger foundation for handling the challenges of your role. Regular physical activity also improves your sleep quality, reduces the risk of chronic illnesses, and boosts your overall resilience.

Mental Health: Guarding Your Mind and Well-Being

In the nonprofit sector, it's easy to become consumed by the mission-driven work you're passionate about. However, the emotional demands of leading a nonprofit can take a toll on your mental health if not carefully managed. Protecting your mental well-being is essential for sustaining your effectiveness as a leader and maintaining a healthy work-life balance.

Here are some strategies for guarding your mental health:

1. Set Boundaries: One of the most important ways to protect your mental health is by setting boundaries between work and personal life. This might mean turning off work emails after a certain time, not checking your phone during family meals, or setting aside specific times for relaxation and self-care. By setting clear boundaries, you create space to recharge and prevent burnout. It's critical to communicate these boundaries to your staff, so they understand when you are available and when you need personal time.

2. Practice Mindfulness: Mindfulness practices, such as meditation, deep breathing, or simply taking a few moments to focus on your surroundings, can help reduce stress and improve mental clarity. Incorporating mindfulness into your daily routine can help you stay grounded and present, even during busy or stressful times. Whether it's a few minutes of deep breathing before a board meeting or a short meditation during lunch, mindfulness can be a powerful tool for managing stress.

3. Seek Support: Don't be afraid to seek support when you need it. This could be talking to a trusted friend or family member, seeking guidance from a mentor, or working with a therapist or counselor. Having a support system in place can provide perspective, encouragement, and a safe space to process your thoughts and emotions. Mental health support is just as important as professional support, and seeking help is a sign of strength, not weakness.

4. Focus on What You Can Control: In the nonprofit world, there will always be challenges and uncertainties. Focus on what you can control, and let go of what you can't. By directing your energy toward actions that are within your control, you can reduce feelings of helplessness and stay more positive and proactive. It's important to recognize that you can't solve every problem, and that's okay.

5. Take Breaks: It's easy to get caught up in the demands of your role and push through without taking breaks. However, regular breaks are essential for maintaining mental clarity and preventing burnout. Step away from your desk, take a short walk, or simply give yourself a few minutes to relax and reset. Even short breaks throughout the day can help you stay focused and energized.

By taking proactive steps to guard your mental health, you'll be better equipped to lead with resilience, empathy, and clarity. Mental well-being is not just about avoiding stress; it's about actively cultivating a sense of peace, balance, and mental fitness.

Emotional Health: Nurturing Relationships and Finding Joy

Emotional well-being is closely tied to your relationships and your ability to find joy and fulfillment outside of work. As a nonprofit CEO, it's important to make time for your loved ones, cultivate meaningful connections, and engage in activities that bring you happiness.

Here are some ways to nurture your emotional health:

1. Prioritize Relationships: Your relationships with family, friends, and loved ones are essential sources of support and joy. Make time for the people who matter most to you, whether it's having dinner with your family, catching up with a friend, or spending quality time with your partner. These relationships provide a sense of belonging and emotional grounding. In moments of stress or uncertainty, these connections remind you of what truly matters.

2. Engage in Activities You Love: Pursuing hobbies and interests outside of work is an important way to nurture your emotional well-being. Whether it's traveling, reading, cooking, or exploring new hobbies, make time for activities that bring you joy and allow you to unwind. Engaging in these activities can provide a much-needed mental break and help you return to work with renewed energy and creativity. Hobbies not only enrich your personal life but also contribute to your overall sense of purpose and satisfaction.

3. Celebrate Small Wins: In the fast-paced world of nonprofit leadership, it's easy to focus on what still needs to be done and overlook the progress you've made. Take time to celebrate small wins—both in your professional and personal life. Recognizing your achievements, no matter how small, can boost your mood and motivation. Celebrate milestones, whether it's successfully completing a project or taking a day off to spend with your family.

4. Find a Mentor: Being a CEO can sometimes feel isolating, especially when you are dealing with difficult decisions or challenges. Finding a mentor can provide valuable support and guidance. Your mentor might be someone in the nonprofit sector or a trusted leader from another field. A mentor can offer perspective, challenge your thinking, and remind you that you don't have to navigate leadership alone.

5. Practice Gratitude: Cultivating a sense of gratitude can have a positive impact on your emotional well-being. Take a few moments each day to reflect on what you're grateful for, whether it's a supportive colleague, a successful project, or a beautiful moment in your personal life. Practicing gratitude can help shift your focus away from stress and challenges and toward the positive aspects of your life. Keeping a gratitude journal or simply taking a few minutes to appreciate the small joys in life can make a significant difference.

6. Seek Balance: Striving for a work-life balance is key to emotional well-being. This doesn't mean that every day will be perfectly balanced, but it's important to regularly assess how you're spending your time and make adjustments as needed. Ensuring that you have

time for both work and personal fulfillment is essential for long-term happiness and success. Remember that balance is an ongoing process, not a destination.

By prioritizing your emotional health, you can lead with greater empathy, creativity, and joy. Emotional well-being allows you to connect more deeply with others, navigate challenges with grace, and sustain the passion and enthusiasm needed for effective leadership.

Self-Care: You Were Hired to Do a Job, Not to Work 24/7

As a nonprofit CEO, you may feel a deep sense of responsibility to your organization, your team, and the people you serve. However, it's important to remember that you were hired to do a job, not to work 24/7. Self-care is not only a personal responsibility but also a professional one. By taking care of yourself, you ensure that you have the energy, focus, and resilience needed to lead effectively.

Here are some strategies for practicing self-care:

1. Use Your Personal Time Off (PTO): Taking time off is essential for recharging and maintaining your well-being. Don't hesitate to use your personal time off (PTO) or vacation days. Whether it's a long weekend, a week-long vacation, or even just a day to relax, time off allows you to step away from work, clear your mind, and return with renewed energy and perspective. Taking time off is a sign of strength, not weakness.

2. Disconnect Regularly: In today's digital age, it can be difficult to fully disconnect from work. However, it's

important to take regular breaks from your devices, especially after work hours and on weekends. Turn off work notifications, avoid checking emails, and give yourself permission to fully disconnect and enjoy your personal time. Set boundaries with your devices to protect your mental space.

3. Delegate and Trust Your Team: As a leader, it's easy to feel like you need to handle everything yourself. However, delegating tasks and trusting your team is not only a way to reduce your workload but also an opportunity to empower your staff. Let go of the need to micromanage and trust that your team can handle their responsibilities. This will free up your time and allow you to focus on the big picture.

4. Set Realistic Expectations: It's important to set realistic expectations for yourself and others. Understand that you can't do everything, and it's okay to say no or delegate tasks when necessary. By setting realistic goals and expectations, you can avoid overcommitting and reduce stress. Recognize that you are only human, and perfection is not the goal.

5. Make Self-Care a Routine: Self-care should be a regular part of your routine, not something you only do when you're feeling burned out. Schedule self-care activities into your week, whether it's a daily meditation practice, a weekly workout, or a monthly massage. Regular self-care helps you maintain your well-being and prevents burnout before it happens.

Getting a Hobby: Finding Joy Outside of Work

Having a hobby or interest outside of work is an important way to find joy, reduce stress, and maintain a healthy work-life balance. Hobbies provide an opportunity to engage in something you're passionate about, explore new interests, and give your mind a break from work-related tasks.

Here's how to find and enjoy a hobby:

1. Explore Your Interests: Think about what activities you enjoy or have always wanted to try. Whether it's painting, gardening, playing a musical instrument, or cooking, explore different hobbies until you find something that resonates with you.

2. Make Time for Your Hobby: Just as you schedule work meetings, schedule time for your hobbies. Whether it's dedicating an hour a day or setting aside time on the weekends, make sure you have regular time to engage in your hobby.

3. Share Your Hobby with Others: Hobbies can be a great way to connect with others who share similar interests. Join a local club, take a class, or participate in group activities related to your hobby. Sharing your hobby with others can provide a sense of community and make the experience even more enjoyable.

4. Find Joy in the Process: The purpose of a hobby is not to achieve perfection but to enjoy the process. Allow yourself to relax and have fun without worrying about the outcome. Whether you're learning a new skill

or simply enjoying a favorite pastime, the goal is to find joy and fulfillment in the activity itself.

5. Use Your Hobby as a Mental Break: Engaging in a hobby allows your mind to focus on something other than work. This mental break can help reduce stress, increase creativity, and improve your overall well-being.

For example, if you enjoy genealogy, as I do, spend time researching your family history, exploring ancestral records, or visiting historical sites. This hobby not only provides a break from work but also offers a sense of connection to the past and a deeper understanding of your heritage. Whether it's genealogy or another passion, the key is to immerse yourself in something that brings you joy.

Taking Care of You as a Nonprofit CEO

As a new nonprofit CEO, it's easy to become consumed by the demands of your role. However, it's essential to remember that taking care of yourself is not only important for your well-being but also for your effectiveness as a leader. By prioritizing your physical, mental, and emotional health, practicing self-care, and finding joy outside of work, you can lead with greater resilience, creativity, and purpose.

Taking care of yourself is an ongoing process, and it requires intentionality and commitment. By making self-care a priority, you'll not only enhance your own well-being but also set a positive example for your team and create a more sustainable and fulfilling work-life balance.

Remember, you were hired to do a job, not to work 24/7. Your organization, your team, and your mission will all benefit from a leader who is healthy, happy, and fully present. Taking care of you is one of the most important investments you can make in your leadership journey.

Chapter 17: Where Do You Go from Here?

As a new nonprofit CEO, you've reached a significant milestone in your career. Leading an organization, especially one with a mission-driven focus, is a tremendous responsibility and a unique opportunity to make a lasting impact. However, reaching the CEO position is not the end of your journey—it's just the beginning of a new chapter. The question now is: Where do you go from here?

When I started my first role as a United Way CEO, someone told me, "Well, there's nowhere to go from here." They meant that, as a CEO, I had reached the pinnacle of my career, with no more promotions to look forward to. At the time, I didn't fully understand that statement. While some might see the CEO role as the final destination, I saw it as a platform for growth, learning, and new challenges. My mind was always thinking, "What else can I do? What's the next opportunity?" And that mindset has guided my journey ever since.

In this chapter, we'll explore the many paths you can take as a nonprofit CEO to continue growing, both personally and professionally. Whether it's seeking out growth opportunities, volunteering in your community, expanding your involvement within your organization's broader network, trying something new, planning for retirement, or simply reading more, there are countless ways to keep moving forward. Let's dive into these avenues and see where they can lead you.

Growth Opportunities: Always Be a Student

One of the most important lessons I've learned in my career is that growth doesn't stop when you become a CEO. In fact, it's more important than ever to continue learning, developing, and expanding your skills. The nonprofit sector is constantly evolving, and as a leader, you need to stay ahead of the curve. This means being a lifelong student—continuously seeking out opportunities to learn, grow, and improve.

Training and Conferences

Training programs and conferences are excellent ways to stay informed about the latest trends, best practices, and innovations in the nonprofit sector. These events provide opportunities to learn from industry experts, network with peers, and gain new insights that you can bring back to your organization. Whether it's a leadership development program, a workshop on fundraising strategies, or a conference on nonprofit governance, investing in your education will pay dividends in your ability to lead effectively.

Look for conferences and training programs that align with your organization's mission and your personal growth goals. Many professional associations offer certifications and specialized training that can enhance your expertise in areas such as finance, human resources, or program evaluation. Additionally, consider attending events outside of your immediate field to gain a broader perspective on leadership and organizational management.

For instance, conferences like the Council on Foundations Annual Conference, BoardSource Leadership Forum, or the Nonprofit Technology Conference are platforms that can introduce you to innovations and strategies that will sharpen your leadership skills. Conferences also create a space for you to meet individuals who are experiencing similar challenges, which can foster a sense of camaraderie and provide you with fresh ideas to bring back to your team.

Leadership Programs

Leadership programs are another valuable resource for nonprofit CEOs. These programs often focus on developing the skills and attributes necessary for effective leadership, such as strategic thinking, emotional intelligence, and decision-making. Participating in a leadership program can also connect you with other leaders, providing a support network and opportunities for collaboration.

Some leadership programs are industry-specific, while others are more general in nature. Both types of programs can be beneficial, offering new perspectives and tools that you can apply to your role as a CEO. Additionally, some programs are designed for executives at different stages of their careers, so you can find a program that meets your current needs and challenges.

For example, the Harvard Kennedy School's Executive Education Programs or the Center for Creative Leadership offer leadership programs tailored to nonprofit executives. These programs allow you to engage with experts and peers on complex topics like nonprofit governance, innovation, and effective fundraising.

Other leadership programs can be run by a local Chamber of Commerce or regional organizations. These programs focus on the local geographic area, but helps prepare participates to learn more about their local area, while grooming them to be leaders in their hometown. These programs usually offer a wonderful way to network and create contacts and friends with individuals you may not have had the chance to interact with on a normal basis.

Formal Education

For those who are particularly ambitious, pursuing formal education is another option. Whether it's a master's degree in nonprofit management, an MBA, or a certificate program in a specialized area, formal education can deepen your knowledge and enhance your credentials. While it requires a significant investment of time and resources, the long-term benefits can be substantial.

If you're considering further education, think about how it aligns with your career goals and the needs of your organization. For example, if you're leading a nonprofit that is expanding internationally, a degree in global studies or international business might be particularly relevant. On the other hand, if your focus is on local community development, a degree in public administration or urban planning could be more applicable.

By continually investing in your own education and skill development, you ensure that you are equipped to navigate the evolving challenges of nonprofit leadership. Moreover, your commitment to personal growth sets a powerful example for your team, inspiring them to pursue their own development.

Volunteering in Your Community: Giving Back and Gaining Perspective

As a nonprofit leader, you're already committed to making a difference in your community. However, it's important to remember that your impact doesn't have to be limited to your role as CEO. Volunteering in your community can provide valuable insights, build relationships, and reinforce your commitment to service.

Volunteering allows you to connect with your community on a more personal level. Whether you're reading to students at a local elementary school, helping with a community clean-up project, or offering your time at a senior home, volunteering can deepen your understanding of the needs and challenges faced by those you serve. It also provides an opportunity to give back in a way that is separate from your professional responsibilities.

Beyond the intrinsic value of giving back, volunteering in different capacities can also make you a more effective leader. Seeing the challenges your beneficiaries face firsthand will give you a renewed perspective that informs how you design programs and lead your team. It's a way of staying connected to the mission at a grassroots level.

In addition to personal satisfaction, these experiences can enhance your leadership skills. Volunteering in settings different from your typical environment can expose you to new ideas, increase your empathy, and help you approach problem-solving from different angles. These qualities are essential for effective leadership and can strengthen your ability to connect with your staff, board members, and stakeholders.

For example, if your organization focuses on food insecurity, spending time volunteering at a local food pantry could give you insights into the day-to-day challenges faced by your community that might not be apparent from behind a desk. By stepping into the volunteer role yourself, you can see how your organization's services are being utilized, what might be improved, and how you can better support your team on the ground.

Volunteering can also be a powerful way to build relationships within your community. By working alongside other volunteers, you can expand your network, collaborate on shared goals, and build a stronger sense of community. These connections can be valuable resources for your organization and can lead to new partnerships, funding opportunities, and support.

Expanding Your Involvement: State, National, and International Footprints

As a nonprofit CEO, your influence and impact can extend beyond your local community. Many organizations have state, national, or even international footprints, offering opportunities for you to get involved at a higher level. Whether it's serving on a large committee, participating in a national coalition, or contributing to an international initiative, expanding your involvement can broaden your horizons and amplify your impact.

Serving on Committees

Serving on committees is an excellent way to contribute your expertise and leadership skills while expanding your network and influence. Many state and national nonprofit organizations have committees focused on specific areas, such as advocacy, governance, or program development. By serving on a committee, you can help shape policies, develop strategies, and make decisions that have a broader impact.

Committee work also provides opportunities to collaborate with other leaders and experts in your field. This collaboration can lead to new ideas, best practices, and innovative solutions that you can bring back to your organization. Additionally, serving on a committee can enhance your visibility and reputation within the nonprofit sector, opening doors to new opportunities and partnerships.

Take, for example, serving on the National Council of Nonprofits' Board of Directors or participating in a state wide chamber initiative. These platforms give you the chance to work on a macro level, influencing policies that affect organizations across the country, while also gaining valuable insights that can benefit your own organization.

National and International Involvement

If your organization has a national or international presence, consider getting involved in broader initiatives or coalitions. National and international involvement allows you to contribute to causes that extend beyond your local community and connect with leaders from diverse backgrounds and regions.

For example, if your organization is part of a national network, you might have the opportunity to participate in national conferences, advocacy efforts, or collaborative projects. These experiences can provide a deeper understanding of the challenges and opportunities facing the nonprofit sector at a larger scale.

Similarly, if your organization has an international footprint, you can explore opportunities to engage with global initiatives, such as humanitarian aid, environmental sustainability, or global health. International involvement can expose you to different cultures, perspectives, and approaches to nonprofit work, enriching your leadership and expanding your impact.

Organizations like The International Society for Third-Sector Research or Care International offer platforms for nonprofit leaders to engage on a global scale, sharing best practices and learning from peers worldwide.

By expanding your involvement beyond your local community, you can contribute to larger efforts, gain new insights, and strengthen your organization's position within the nonprofit sector.

Trying Something New: Embracing Innovation and Change

As a nonprofit CEO, it's important to stay open to new ideas, approaches, and opportunities. The nonprofit sector is constantly evolving, and organizations that embrace innovation and change are better positioned to thrive in a rapidly changing environment.

Embracing Innovation

Innovation is not just about adopting new technologies or launching new programs—it's about being open to new ways of thinking and doing things. As a leader, you have the opportunity to foster a culture of innovation within your organization by encouraging creativity, experimentation, and continuous improvement.

One way to embrace innovation is by being willing to try new approaches to problem-solving. Whether it's implementing new fundraising strategies, exploring new partnerships, or rethinking how your programs are delivered, innovation requires a willingness to take risks and learn from failure. By creating an environment where innovation is valued and supported, you can inspire your team to think outside the box and develop solutions that drive your organization forward.

Take, for example, the increasing use of impact investing in the nonprofit world. Impact investing, where an organization seeks both social and financial returns, might be an innovative approach your nonprofit can explore. By trying something new and aligning it with your mission, you could open up new funding streams and create lasting change in ways that traditional grants may not.

Exploring New Opportunities

In addition to fostering innovation within your organization, it's important to stay open to new opportunities for growth and development. This might mean taking on new challenges, pursuing new initiatives, or exploring new career paths.

For example, you might consider expanding your organization's programs to reach new populations or address emerging needs. This could involve launching a new initiative, forming a strategic partnership, or developing a new revenue stream. By staying open to new opportunities, you can position your organization to adapt to changing circumstances and continue making a meaningful impact.

Similarly, you might explore new opportunities for your own professional growth. This could involve taking on a new leadership role within your organization, exploring a different sector, or even considering a new career path. By remaining open to change and new experiences, you can continue to grow as a leader and find new ways to contribute to the causes you care about.

Planning for Retirement: Preparing for Your Next Chapter

As a nonprofit CEO, you may not be thinking about retirement just yet, but it's never too early to start planning for your next chapter. Whether you envision retiring at 55 and moving to Florida or continuing to work into your 60s, 70s or longer, while pursuing personal passions, having a plan in place will help you transition smoothly and ensure that your retirement is fulfilling and rewarding.

Setting Retirement Goals

The first step in planning for retirement is setting clear goals. Think about when you want to retire, what you want to do in retirement, and how you want to spend your time. Do you see yourself traveling, volunteering, pursuing hobbies, or spending more time with family? Having a clear vision of what you want to achieve in retirement will help guide your planning and decision-making.

Consider both your financial and personal goals. Financially, you'll need to ensure that you have the resources to support your desired lifestyle in retirement. This might involve working with a financial planner, contributing to retirement accounts, and making investments that align with your long-term goals.

On a personal level, think about how you want to stay active and engaged in retirement. For many nonprofit leaders, retirement doesn't mean stepping away from service altogether—it might involve volunteering, mentoring, or even serving on nonprofit boards. By planning ahead, you can ensure that your retirement is both fulfilling and purposeful.

Creating a Succession Plan

Part of planning for retirement is creating a succession plan for your organization. As a CEO, it's important to ensure that your organization is prepared for a smooth leadership transition when the time comes. This involves identifying and developing potential leaders within your organization, creating a clear plan for the transition, and communicating your plans to your board and key stakeholders.

A well-thought-out succession plan will help ensure that your organization continues to thrive after you retire and that your legacy is preserved. It also provides peace of mind, knowing that your organization is in good hands and that you can move on to your next chapter with confidence.

Leaders Are Readers: The Power of Continuous Learning

As a nonprofit CEO, one of the best ways to continue growing and developing as a leader is through reading. Books provide a wealth of knowledge, inspiration, and new perspectives that can enhance your leadership skills and broaden your understanding of the world.

The Importance of Reading

Reading is a powerful tool for personal and professional growth. It allows you to learn from the experiences of others, gain new insights into leadership and management, and stay informed about trends and developments in your field. Whether you're reading a leadership book, a biography, or a novel, the act of reading can stimulate your mind, spark new ideas, and help you think more critically and creatively.

For example, every year, Bill Gates shares his list of books he's reading or plans to read over the summer. His list typically includes a mix of books on leadership, industry-specific topics, and historical biographies. This approach to reading—combining professional development with personal interest—can provide a well-rounded perspective that enriches your leadership.

Building Your Reading List

As a leader, it's important to be intentional about what you read. Consider building a reading list that includes a variety of genres and topics. Here are some categories to consider:

- Leadership and Management: Books on leadership and management can provide valuable insights and tools for leading your organization. Look for books that offer practical advice, case studies, and thought-provoking ideas.

- Industry-Specific Books: Stay informed about developments in the nonprofit sector by reading books that are specific to your industry. This might include books on fundraising, governance, program evaluation, or social impact.

- Biographies and Memoirs: Biographies and memoirs of influential leaders can provide inspiration and lessons in resilience, innovation, and vision. Learning about the experiences of others can help you navigate challenges and find new ways to lead.

- Fiction and Literature: Don't overlook the value of fiction and literature. Reading novels, short stories, and poetry can help you develop empathy, improve your communication skills, and stimulate your creativity.

- Personal Interests: Finally, include books that align with your personal interests. Whether it's history, science, travel, or philosophy, reading about topics you're passionate about can provide a welcome break from work and contribute to your overall well-being.

By making reading a regular part of your routine, you can continue to learn, grow, and develop as a leader.

My Dad's Wisdom: A Simple but Powerful Guide

I'd like to close this chapter with a piece of wisdom from my father, who was my first and greatest mentor. For my office, he told me to always have three books on my desk: a Bible, the Boy Scout Handbook, and a dictionary. He shared that most of life's problems and issues could be found in those three books.

While these books don't provide direct answers to financial questions or how to improve a specific program, they offer something just as important: perspective. The Bible offers spiritual guidance and moral principles, the Boy Scout Handbook teaches practical skills and values, and the dictionary is a tool for understanding and communication. Together, they represent a balanced approach to life and leadership—grounded in faith, practicality, and knowledge.

As you continue your journey as a nonprofit CEO, remember that leadership is not just about making decisions and achieving goals. It's about staying grounded, seeking wisdom, and finding balance in all aspects of your life. Thanks, Dad, for this timeless advice.

The Journey Continues

As a new nonprofit CEO, you've already accomplished a great deal, but your journey is far from over. Where do you go from here? The possibilities are endless. By seeking out growth opportunities, giving back to your community, expanding your involvement, embracing innovation, planning for retirement, and continuing to learn and grow, you can keep moving forward, both personally and professionally.

Remember, leadership is not a destination—it's a continuous journey of growth, learning, and service. Keep challenging yourself, stay open to new experiences, and never stop striving to be the best leader you can be. Your organization, your community, and your legacy will all be richer for it.

Conclusion: Navigating the Journey of Nonprofit Leadership

As you stand at the threshold of your journey as a nonprofit CEO, it's essential to reflect on the path that lies ahead. Over the years, I've had countless conversations with new CEOs and those considering this professional path, often over the phone or while sharing a cup of coffee. The topics within this book stem from these heartfelt discussions, shaped by the questions, challenges, and insights shared by those embarking on a similar journey. My hope is that the knowledge and guidance offered here will serve as a steady compass, helping you navigate your own path with confidence and clarity.

The chapters of this book have equipped you with the foundational knowledge, skills, and insights necessary to lead a nonprofit organization successfully. From understanding the intricate nature of nonprofits and the roles and responsibilities of a CEO to mastering fundraising, financial management, and the art of leadership, you now possess a comprehensive toolkit. These tools will be your companions as you take on the daily challenges and the overarching strategic goals that come with leading a nonprofit.

However, being a nonprofit CEO is about more than just ticking off boxes and executing duties. It's about transformation—both for the organization and yourself. The conclusion of this book is not just a summary of what you've learned but a call to action. It's a reminder that the real work begins now, and that your leadership has the potential to make a profound impact on the people and communities you serve.

The Essence of Nonprofit Leadership

At its core, nonprofit leadership is about more than managing resources, meeting fundraising goals, or overseeing daily operations. It's about driving a mission, creating a vision for the future, and inspiring others to join you on that journey. As a nonprofit CEO, you are entrusted with the responsibility of stewarding an organization that often serves as a lifeline for those in need. Your decisions will affect not only the financial health of your organization but also the lives of countless individuals who rely on the services and programs you provide.

Throughout this book, we've explored the many facets of nonprofit leadership—from building strong relationships with your board, staff, and community to understanding the intricacies of your organization's financials. These are critical skills, but they represent only part of what it takes to succeed. The other part is less tangible but just as crucial: your passion, your commitment, and your ability to lead with empathy and integrity. These personal qualities will define your success as a CEO and determine the impact you can make on your organization and community.

Embracing Change and Innovation

The nonprofit sector is constantly evolving. New challenges emerge, funding landscapes shift, and the needs of the communities you serve change over time. As a nonprofit CEO, adaptability is essential. You must be ready to embrace change and seek out innovative solutions to the problems you face. This doesn't just mean keeping up with trends or adopting new technologies—it requires a mindset of continuous learning and a willingness to take calculated risks.

Innovation in the nonprofit world goes beyond surface-level changes. It means rethinking how your organization operates and how it can best fulfill its mission in an ever-changing world. Innovation might be about introducing new programs that better address the evolving needs of your beneficiaries, or it could involve reimagining how you fundraise in a digital age. Often, the best ideas come from within your organization or from the communities you serve. As a CEO, fostering a culture of openness to new ideas and solutions is critical. By creating an environment where innovation is encouraged, you ensure that your organization remains relevant, impactful, and resilient.

The Power of Relationships

A recurring theme in this book has been the importance of relationships. Whether you are engaging with your board, staff, donors, volunteers, or the broader community, your success as a nonprofit CEO will be largely determined by your ability to build and maintain strong relationships. Leadership in the nonprofit sector is collaborative by nature. While you are at the helm, steering the ship, you rely on the efforts and support of a diverse group of stakeholders to achieve your goals.

Building strong relationships requires more than good communication skills—it requires trust, transparency, and a genuine commitment to collaboration. It's about understanding that your leadership is not a solo endeavor. The success of your organization depends on the collective efforts of everyone involved, from the frontline staff delivering services to the donors writing checks in support of your mission.

As CEO, you must foster a sense of shared purpose and mutual respect. This involves not only leading from the front but also empowering others to lead in their areas of expertise. By doing so, you create a strong, supportive network that will help your organization thrive and sustain its mission over time.

Leading with Integrity

Integrity is the bedrock of effective nonprofit leadership. Throughout your career as a CEO, you will face difficult decisions, and your choices will be scrutinized by many—your board, staff, donors, and the public. It's crucial that you lead with honesty, transparency, and a commitment to ethical principles. Every decision you make must be grounded in what's best for your organization, its mission, and the communities it serves.

Leading with integrity means holding yourself accountable for your actions and decisions. It also means being mindful of the trust that has been placed in you by your stakeholders. Ethical leadership isn't just about following the rules; it's about being deeply attuned to the impact of your actions on the people you serve. When your leadership is guided by strong ethical principles, you build trust and credibility, which are essential to the long-term success of your organization.

Moreover, leading with integrity requires that you remain true to your own values. The path of leadership is fraught with challenges, and there will be times when you are tempted to compromise in the face of external pressures or short-term goals. But holding fast to your values, even in the face of adversity, is what will set you apart as a leader and leave a lasting positive legacy.

The Importance of Self-Care

One of the greatest challenges of nonprofit leadership is balancing your many responsibilities without burning out. The pressures of running an organization, managing relationships, securing funding, and delivering on your mission can easily become overwhelming. But as we discussed in Chapter 16, self-care is not a luxury—it is a necessity for long-term success.

Leadership is a marathon, not a sprint. To sustain your energy, passion, and effectiveness, you must make time to rest, reflect, and recharge. This requires setting boundaries, both in your professional and personal life. It means giving yourself permission to step away from work when necessary and seeking out support when you need it.

Remember that your well-being is closely tied to the well-being of your organization. When you take care of yourself, you are better equipped to care for others and lead your organization effectively. Leading by example in this regard can also have a profound impact on your team. By prioritizing self-care, you model healthy work habits and create a culture where employees feel empowered to take care of themselves as well.

Measuring Success: Beyond the Numbers

In the nonprofit sector, success is often measured by tangible metrics—dollars raised, programs delivered, and people served. While these numbers are important, they don't tell the whole story of your organization's impact. As a CEO, you must look beyond the numbers to truly understand and measure the success of your organization.

Ask yourself: Are we making a meaningful difference in the lives of the people we serve? Are we contributing to lasting, systemic change in our community? Are we fulfilling our mission in a way that aligns with our values and long-term vision? These are the questions that should guide your leadership.

In Chapter 11, we discussed the importance of driving and demonstrating success. As you move forward in your role, keep in mind that success is not just about achieving short-term goals; it's about building a sustainable, impactful organization that will continue to make a difference for years to come.

Looking Ahead: Your Legacy as a Nonprofit CEO

As you continue on your journey as a nonprofit CEO, it's important to consider the legacy you want to leave behind. What kind of impact do you want to have on your organization, your community, and the nonprofit sector as a whole? How will you ensure that your organization continues to thrive even after you've moved on? What values and principles will guide your leadership?

Your legacy as a nonprofit CEO will be shaped by the choices you make, the relationships you build, and the impact you create. By leading with integrity, embracing innovation, prioritizing relationships, and taking care of yourself, you will create a legacy that reflects your deep commitment to making a difference. And ultimately, the true measure of your legacy will not be in the accolades you receive but in the lives you've touched, the communities you've served, and the lasting change you've helped create.

This is Just the Beginning

The conclusion of this book marks the beginning of your journey as a nonprofit CEO. The path ahead will be filled with both challenges and opportunities for growth. As you move forward, remember the lessons you've learned in these chapters, and let them guide you as you lead your organization with vision and purpose.

You have the potential to make a profound difference in the world through your work. By staying true to your mission, leading with integrity, fostering collaboration and innovation, and prioritizing self-care, you will build a resilient and impactful organization that serves its community well.

The journey of nonprofit leadership is not always easy, but it is deeply rewarding. As you take on this vital role, know that you have the tools, knowledge, and passion to succeed. Now, it's time to put those tools to work — to lead with purpose, vision, and a commitment to making a lasting impact.

Your journey as a nonprofit CEO is just beginning. The impact you can make is limitless. Lead with courage, compassion, and integrity, and you will leave a legacy that will inspire others for years to come. Thank you for your commitment to making a difference. Enjoy the journey.

About the Author

With over 25 years of experience as a transformational leader, Alan H. Turner II has made a significant impact in the nonprofit sector. His extensive expertise spans nonprofit and association management, community engagement, fundraising, team building, social media strategy, and public policy. Alan's unwavering dedication to advancing nonprofit missions has led to the successful raising of nearly $300 million, strategically invested in health and human service programs that have positively impacted the lives of more than eight million individuals and families.

Alan has held the position of President and CEO for four local United Ways across the United States, serving communities in South Dakota, Florida, Alabama, and Tennessee. Under his leadership, these organizations achieved record-setting annual fundraising campaigns, reached critical community impact goals, and navigated successfully through times of crisis. He also significantly increased the visibility and relevance of these United Way organizations through innovative community engagement and social media strategies. Alan's leadership acumen earned him the opportunity to participate in United Way

Worldwide's prestigious Advanced Leadership Program and Executive Leadership Development Program.

Beyond his leadership roles with United Way, Alan has contributed his talents to some of the most respected nonprofits and associations in the world, including St. Jude Children's Research Hospital and the American Red Cross. Earlier in his career, he led the Association of New York State Youth Bureaus, served as Managing Director of the United States Practical Shooting Association, worked with the New York State Assembly, and was deeply involved with the Boy Scouts of America.

Alan holds an M.B.A. from Union University in Jackson, TN, and a B.S. in Business Administration from Daemen College (now Daemen University) in Amherst, NY, where he was honored as a Distinguished Alumni in 2011. He proudly serves on the university's Board of Trustees. Alan also holds an A.A.S. degree from S.U.N.Y. Cobleskill and began doctoral studies at Southeastern University in Lakeland, FL. Further demonstrating his commitment to continued learning and leadership development, Alan has completed executive education programs at Harvard Business School, the Harvard Kennedy School, and the Kellogg School of Management. Additionally, he has participated in several local leadership development programs.

A proud veteran, Alan served honorably in the U.S. Army Reserves with the 338th General Hospital Reserve Unit in Niagara Falls, New York.

Originally from upstate New York, Alan was raised as a proud Army brat and has lived in various communities across the United States. He now resides just outside Denver, Colorado, with his wife, Stephanie, and their children, Andrew and Sara. He enjoys traveling, touring historical locations, is an avid genealogist, and is always on the lookout for new coffee spots and microbreweries. Alan also has a long-standing tradition of collecting comic books with his son, particularly early issues of X-Men and Captain America, and places a high value on spending quality time with his family. Deeply committed to his Christian faith, Alan seeks to integrate his values into his professional and personal life.

Alan continues to mentor individuals across the country in their career pursuits and works closely with nonprofit organizations. He remains actively involved in a wide range of community and civic organizations, driven by his passion for service and his commitment to building stronger, healthier communities.

You may contact Alan at www.AHTurner2.com

www.ingramcontent.com/pod-product-compliance
Lightning Source LLC
Chambersburg PA
CBHW031621210526
45464CB00004B/1691